By Faith

LIVING IN THE CERTAINTY OF GOD'S REALITY

JOHN FRANKLIN & LONNIE RILEY

D1511690

LifeWay Press®
Nashville, Tennessee

ISBN 1-4158-2582-3

This book is the resource for course CG-1193
in the subject area Bible Studies in the Christian Growth Study Plan.

Dewey Decimal classification: 234.2
Subject headings: FAITH \ CHRISTIAN LIFE

Unless otherwise noted, all Scripture quotations are taken from the
Holman Christian Standard Bible®, copyright © 1999, 2000, 2001, 2002, 2003
by Holman Bible Publishers. Used by permission.
Scripture quotations marked NKJV are from the New King James Version.
Copyright © 1979, 1980, 1982, Thomas Nelson, Inc., Publishers.

We believe that the Bible has God for its author; salvation for its end;
and truth, without any mixture of error, for its matter and that
all Scripture is totally true and trustworthy. The 2000 statement
of *The Baptist Faith and Message* is our doctrinal guideline.

To order additional copies of this resource, write
to LifeWay Church Resources Customer Service;
One LifeWay Plaza; Nashville, TN 37234-0113;
phone toll free (800) 458-2772; e-mail *orderentry@lifeway.com;*
fax (615) 251-5933; order online at *www.lifeway.com;*
or visit the LifeWay Christian Store serving you.

Printed in the United States of America

Leadership and Adult Publishing
LifeWay Church Resources
One LifeWay Plaza
Nashville, TN 37234-0175

Contents

The Authors

John Franklin is the pastor of Woodmont Bible Church in Nashville, Tennessee. He previously served in several other church positions and at LifeWay Christian Resources as a prayer specialist in the discipleship and pastoral areas. His other books include *A House of Prayer: Prayer Ministries for Your Church, And the Place Was Shaken: How to Lead a Powerful Prayer Meeting,* and *Spiritual Warfare: Biblical Truth for Victory.*

John received his bachelor's degree from Samford University, his master of divinity from the Southern Baptist Theological Seminary, and his doctor of ministry from Beeson Divinity School. He and his wife, Kathy, have three children—Daniel, Nathan, and Susanna.

Lonnie Riley and his wife, Belinda, are the founders of Meridzo Center Ministries, Inc., in the Appalachian Mountains of southeastern Kentucky. Lonnie responded to God's call to serve the people of the region through a ministry using the faith principles he shares in this book. He has additionally served as the assistant director of evangelism for the State Convention of Baptists in Ohio; as the assistant to the president of the University of the Cumberlands; and as the pastor of churches in Ohio, Kentucky, and Mississippi.

Lonnie received an associate of arts in civil engineering from the University of Kentucky, Southeast Campus; received a bachelor of arts from the University of the Cumberlands; and did further study at the Southern Baptist Theological Seminary.

Lonnie and Belinda have three grown children—Lisa, Brian and Amy. They also have six grandchildren—Allisa, Gabriel, Jesika, Gavin, Macie, and Gracen.

John and Lonnie co-wrote the content of *By Faith.* John also wrote the learning activities and the leader guide.

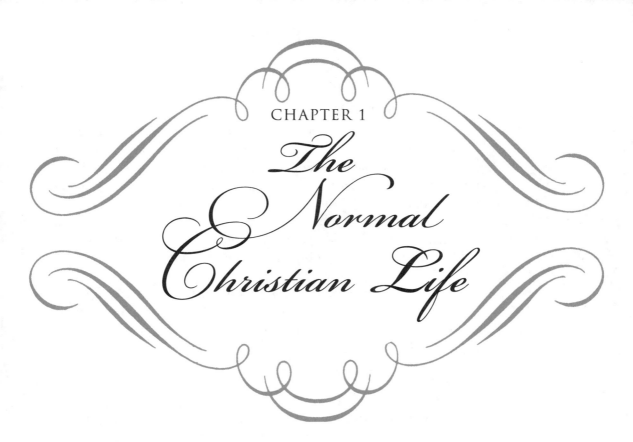

CHAPTER 1

The Normal Christian Life

Let's begin with a personal question. Are you normal or weird? Do you fit in, or are you just a little strange? Before you answer, think about this: how would you know that you were normal or weird? In the past a minority of people have put on weird clothes and somehow persuaded a whole culture to do the same. Yet others did strange things and were ostracized. Nobody wanted to imitate them.

Being normal also suffers from this schizophrenic standard. Some cultures have made uniformity a virtue, but in America our rugged individualism disdains normality. Yes, oddly enough, both weird and normal can be perceived as positive or negative. So how do you know what you really are and whether it's good or bad?

Your answer to that depends on who defines the standards of weird and normal. If you've ever flipped through old high-school yearbooks to observe fashion trends or if you've scanned several decades of values in a culture, you may have noticed that when people set the standard, it inevitably changes. In contrast, Christians look to God, who does not change, to define what is normal and weird. The Bible pictures *normal* as a lifestyle that conforms to the way God designed a relationship with Him to work, while weird is a lifestyle that does not match His intention. So let's ask the original question with a twist. By God's standard, are you normal or weird? Does your relationship with Him function the way He intended it to work?

> The Bible pictures normal as a lifestyle that conforms to the way God designed a relationship with Him to work.

1. Before answering, consider the significance of your reply. List three things in your life that will be affected by the degree to which you conform to God's standard.

1. _____
2. _____
3. _____

Now mark the number on the scale that represents your conformity to God's standard for a life that honors Him.

1	2	3	4	5	6	7	8	9	10

Weird   Normal

You could have included any number of things on your list that will be affected by your conformity to God's standard, such as your level of intimacy with Him, how much He uses you, and what kind of reward you will have in eternity. Both in this life and the life to come, knowing how God intended a relationship with Him to work will affect major dimensions of our lives. On a scale of 1 to 10, the weight of being normal from God's perspective is a 10. Maybe you had trouble ranking yourself because you wondered, *What would normal look like?* That's a good question.

What Is Normal?

In school many students who want to save time in study preparation turn to CliffsNotes®. These notes briefly summarize the most important facts about a book or a subject. Although they leave out many enriching details, they list the main point of the work, thereby giving a student an understanding of the essential facts. God has given us one chapter in the New Testament that condenses a huge portion of the Old Testament, a kind of biblical CliffsNotes. It lists a wide spectrum of biblical figures who were commended by God and identifies the one criterion for which all of them received that commendation. In short, it defines *normal* from God's perspective.

2. Read Hebrews 11 and identify what characterized all of these relationships with God: _____

Write the number of times the phrase *by faith* occurs: _____

Depending on your translation, you probably saw the phrase *by faith* 18 or 19 times. The word *faith* itself occurs 24 times in Greek in the chapter. If you are like most people, you do not have to be told something that many times to get the point! Why did the writer of Hebrews indulge in such overkill? Because his people's relationships with God hung in the balance. His flock felt the biting winds of persecution blowing, and they teetered on the brink of giving up (see Heb. 10:38). The author flung himself into this letter to arrest their dangerous drift toward the falls of self-destruction. You can almost sense that his words were moistened by the drops of his perspiration. This truth proved so colossal, so vital, that he labored intensely to hammer its pylons deep into the foundations of their hearts. The thud of his first blow rings out: "By faith Abel. ..." Again he strikes: "By faith, Enoch. ..." His peals continue: "By faith Noah ... by faith Abraham ... by faith Sarah ... by faith ... by faith ... by faith ..." (Heb. 11:4-5,7-8,11,17,20-21).

This repetition was the literary equivalent of doing backflips, shouting in a megaphone, or blowing a bullhorn—whatever the writer could do to seize his readers' attention. They must get it. The Old Testament CliffsNotes cry out that *normal* from God's perspective is this: everyone approved by God conducted his or her relationship with Him by faith! No exception exists in Scripture. The author ended the chapter by making the point again, stating that time failed him "to tell about Gideon, Barak, Samson, Jephthah, of David and Samuel and the prophets" (Heb. 11:32), who all lived by faith as well. We could easily add New Testament characters to the list—John the Baptist; the twelve disciples; the centurion; the Syro-

"My righteous one will live by faith; and if he draws back, My soul has no pleasure in him."
Hebrews 10:38

Phoenecian woman; a host of people healed in the Gospels; Jesus' followers in the upper room; Stephen; Paul; and others throughout the Book of Acts, the Letters, and Revelation. As far as biblical characters were concerned, *normal* was *consistently walking in a faith relationship with God to impact their world.*

3. Does God expect us to walk with Him in the same manner?
○ Yes   ○ No   **State the reason for your answer.**

God still expects us to walk with Him by faith.

If the pattern of history and God's present-day activity are any indication, God still expects us to walk with Him by faith. The testimonies of the early church fathers in the second, third, and fourth centuries demonstrate this fact. Saint Patrick in the fifth century was known for his incredible faith; through his influence the whole of Ireland turned to God. In the 1200s Saint Francis of Assisi rejected his sin, his father's wealth, and the norms of the day. Giving away all he had, he began an itinerant ministry that profoundly impacted Europe. The Reformation sparked by Martin Luther had as one of its three bases *sola fide*—faith alone. Great missionaries such as William Carey and Hudson Taylor conducted their ministries by faith. Through them India and China opened to the Christian gospel in unprecedented ways. The list could go on, but let's focus on two examples.

In the 1800s a young man in Bristol, England, named George Mueller became burdened that very few Christians around him demonstrated faith in God in their everyday lives. They would say things like "Of course, you must have faith, but you can't run a business that way" and "We need to have faith, but we must be practical as well." Mueller prayed and asked the Lord if He would make his life an example of faith to encourage others that God was as real in his day as He was in the Bible. God led Mueller to start an orphanage founded on two conditions: he could never publicize his needs, and he could never solicit money. He must pray for provision so that when God provided, everyone would know that He was real. When George Mueller died in 1895, he had reared more than 10,000 orphans and had received the equivalent of more than one hundred million dollars in today's currency. His meticulous journal of his prayer requests recorded more than 50,000 answers to prayer.

During World War II the Germans incarcerated a 52-year-old Dutch woman named Corrie ten Boom in the dreaded concentration camp of Ravensbruck. Daily she was forced to witness abuse and death. She suffered unrelenting hunger, cold, disease, and cruelty. She watched the insatiable crematorium continually belch smoke as it devoured its victims' bodies. Such an existence usually killed the soul of the living long before the body followed; yet in the midst of this nightmare God spoke to ten Boom. She sensed that after the war God would use her to tell others of Christ. After her release this unassuming former watchmaker began traveling the world with her message. With no credentials, friends, or resources she simply obeyed God, trusting Him for every need. God began dramatically opening doors in the most unlikely ways. He financially provided for her time and again, although she never asked for a penny. At times she went to a country without a person to meet or a place to stay, but when she arrived, God connected her with someone and revealed the reason He had sent her. Corrie ten Boom lived to age 91, speaking in more than 60 countries, colaboring with the greatest Christian leaders of her day, and leading countless thousands to the Lord.

4. These are examples of very well-known Christians. Does God use ordinary people like this today?

○ No, only really spiritual people can walk with God by faith.

○ I don't know, but I'd like to know if it's possible for God to use me that way.

○ Yes, He does. Their lives may look different from Mueller and ten Boom, but He will use anyone who is willing to radically trust Him.

The stories of George Mueller and Corrie ten Boom are widely known because of the degree to which God worked in them. However, God used them, not because they were more spiritual than other people but because of their faith. God works the same way today through ordinary people. A man in a 16-member church led hundreds in his state to become involved in disaster-relief ministry. God used another to start a racetrack ministry. Another provides Bibles for immigrants. Another sent seven airplanes of clothes and supplies to an orphanage in Romania. God used still another to minister to women who were reentering life after leaving prison. None of

God works the same way today through ordinary people.

these people were ordained ministers or superspiritual Christians. They were all ordinary people. But each person needed faith in order to be used by God. Whether you are an orphanage director, a concentration-camp survivor, or an average person in the pew, the normal way God expects you to conduct your relationship with Him is by faith. From God's perspective, the normal life is a life of faith.

5. Give three examples that illustrate God's standard of what is normal, along with the world's contrasting idea.

God's Way   The World's Way

1. _____   _____
2. _____   _____
3. _____   _____

God Desires a Faith Relationship with You

God could have designed a relationship with Him to work in any number of ways. He could have selected intelligence as the basis of that relationship. He could have required works, effort, self-denial, or performance. However, He bypassed all of these criteria. Because our perfect God has perfect knowledge, it was impossible for Him to choose a less-than-perfect basis for us to relate to Him. God designed His way of relating to us to produce what is best for us, to accomplish what He wants to do through us, and to bring glory to Himself.

God designed His way of relating to us to produce what is best for us, to accomplish what He wants to do through us, and to bring glory to Himself.

6. Why do you think God chose faith as the foundation of a relationship with Himself?
○ Faith requires greater dependence, thereby keeping me closer to God.
○ My love for Him increases when I risk all I am and He comes through for me.
○ His glory is more plainly revealed to everyone when He does what only He can do.
○ Faith can be exercised equally well by a person with a Ph.D. or by someone who is mentally handicapped, thereby leveling the playing field before Him.
○ All of the above

Following God by faith creates advantages that other ways of relating to Him could not. Faith requires dependence on Him that keeps us close, increases our love, reveals His glory more plainly, and produces a host of other benefits. Therefore, when God calls us into a relationship, He immediately begins working in our lives to train us to walk with Him by faith. Just as we begin our relationship with Him by faith, we continue walking with Him by faith throughout life. Just how intensely God desires this kind of relationship can be seen in the following three truths.

Jesus began training His disciples to walk by faith the moment He called them. The Gospel of Mark records the Lord's call to Peter, Andrew, James, and John by the Sea of Galilee to follow Him. Bound up in His command was a call to walk with Him, experience Him, and be used by Him. Everything Jesus intended for their whole lives, He packaged into one simple statement.

7. See if you can finish the verse without looking in the margin: "Follow Me, and I will make you _____."

Most believers would answer *fishers of men*, but Jesus literally said in Greek, "I will make you *become* fishers of men." Several Bible translations omit the word *become* to make the statement more closely resemble the way we talk. But the presence of the Greek word *genesthai*, an infinitive meaning *to become*, indicates that "fishers of men" was the end result of Jesus' training. *To become* was the process of transformation resulting from the training. In other words, Jesus was saying, "Peter, Andrew, James, and John, if you will follow Me the next few years of your lives, I will take you through a discipleship process that will radically transform you. When I finish with you, you will have become the kind of men who will turn the world upside down. You will know how to walk with God by faith in such a way that He will use you to bring thousands of people into His kingdom." When you read the Gospels, notice the process Jesus used to mold His followers. The Gospel accounts are a record of the process by which God takes ordinary people and radically transforms them in such a way that God can do anything He wants through them as they respond to Him in faith.

"Jesus said to them, 'Follow Me, and I will make you become fishers of men.'" Mark 1:17, NKJV

11

The before-and-after pictures of Jesus' disciples illustrate just how radical their transformation was. The track record of their discipleship process is strewn with failures. Peter sank in the water (see Matt. 14:29-30). James and John urged Jesus to call down fire from heaven on the offending Samaritans (see Luke 9:54-55). They counseled Jesus to send away the five thousand (see Matt. 14:15). They tried to prohibit children from coming to Jesus (see Matt. 19:13). They couldn't cast out a demon (see Matt. 17:19-21). But after Jesus had finished with them, they were the heroes of Acts who preached at Pentecost (see Acts 2:14-40), stood up to the Sanhedrin (see Acts 4:13-20), resolved church conflict (see Acts 15:1-35), oversaw the revival in Samaria (see Acts 8:14-17), and won a host of other victories. Their spiritual anemia in the Gospels was replaced by a dynamic walk with God that earned them the reputation of turning the world upside down (see Acts 17:6). What a transformation!

The most astounding reality in these before-and-after pictures is not the disciples but Jesus. What did He do over three years that caused these men to walk by faith? What did He teach, what did He emphasize, how did He train them to so radically transform them? Sometimes Christians sheepishly identify with the disciples in the Gospels, saying things such as "You know, sometimes I feel just like Peter, putting my foot in my mouth" or "Boy, they sure were slow. I'm so slow sometimes too." Although we have all experienced failure, we must keep in mind that this stage lasted only a few dozen months in the lives of Jesus' disciples. The Gospels do not set the standard for their walk of faith; the Book of Acts does. Knowing what Jesus did to build His disciples' faith is extremely important because He has not changed His methods. He never turns to His Father and says, "You know, Father, now that I've had two thousand years to think it over, I believe I can improve on My discipleship process. I have a brand-new program I want You to look at so that We can do it differently now." On the contrary, the training Jesus used with His closest followers is the same process He uses to make people of faith today. We can get a clear picture of His training process by examining Scripture to observe how He worked with His disciples—where He began, what He rewarded, what He corrected, and what He highlighted as teaching points.

The training Jesus used with His closest followers is the same process He uses to make people of faith today.

8. As you read the following verses, underline what Jesus affirmed and circle what He rebuked.

"If that's how God clothes the grass of the field, which is here today and thrown into the furnace tomorrow, won't He do much more for you—you of little faith?" (Matt. 6:30).

"Hearing this, Jesus was amazed and said to those following Him, 'I assure you: I have not found anyone in Israel with so great a faith!'" (Matt. 8:10).

"He said to them, 'Why are you fearful, you of little faith?' Then He got up and rebuked the winds and the sea. And there was a great calm" (Matt. 8:26).

"Jesus turned and saw her. 'Have courage, daughter,' He said. 'Your faith has made you well.' And the woman was made well from that moment" (Matt. 9:22).

"Immediately Jesus reached out His hand, caught hold of him, and said to him, 'You of little faith, why did you doubt?'" (Matt. 14:31).

"Jesus replied to her, 'Woman, your faith is great. Let it be done for you as you want.' And from that moment her daughter was cured" (Matt. 15:28).

"Aware of this, Jesus said, 'You of little faith! Why are you discussing among yourselves that you do not have bread?'" (Matt. 16:8).

Jesus zealously highlighted and exalted people who had faith. Did you notice that He especially commended to His disciples the centurion (see Matt. 8:10), the woman with an issue of blood (9:22), and the woman with a demon-possessed daughter (15:28) as examples? Did you notice that four times He rebuked His disciples for their "little faith"? He constantly reinforced faith in God regardless of the circumstance, challenge, or storm. This pattern, its frequency, and its intensity reveal the high value God places on faith and His passion for us to relate to Him by faith.

Jesus zealously highlighted and exalted people who had faith.

God connects His work in and through your life to your faith. Another way God encourages us to relate to Him by faith is the connection He established between our faith and His work in our lives. One indication of this connection is the phrase Jesus often used, "according to your faith." For those who have known Bible stories for a long time, sometimes the shock wears off. However, those who walked with Jesus lived in a constant state of astonishment (see Mark 1:27; 2:12; 6:51; 9:15; 10:32; 16:8). Many times that shock occurred because of His miracles, but often His teaching drew this same wonder (see Mark 1:22; 6:2; 10:24,26; 11:18). No doubt His teaching on faith generated many occasions for His hearers' mouths to drop open. In the Old Testament God all but ignored the subject of faith. Although the Old Testament constitutes 75 percent of the Bible, it contains only 4 of the 234 verses that use the word *faith*. We certainly recognize the many great figures before Christ who functioned by faith, but the old covenant was founded on works. When Jesus came, He made a radical shift to a new covenant based on faith. This new emphasis would have caught them off guard, especially when He began to do what He did in the account in the margin.

> **9. Read Matthew 9:27-30 in the margin and identify the factor that invited God's work in the blind men's lives.**
> ○ Their need ○ Their sincerity ○ Their faith
> ○ Their fervency ○ Their righteousness

Jesus already knew what He was going to do with the blind men. He set up this healing as an object lesson for His disciples. He asked the blind men only one question: "Do you believe that I can do this?" (v. 28). Of course, Jesus wasn't fishing for information; He already knew the answer. He merely wanted them to understand on what basis He would work in their lives—according to their faith. He linked His activity in their lives with their faith, not with their need, their fervency, their sincerity, or their righteousness. Throughout the Gospels Jesus repeatedly emphasized faith as the one requirement for God's work in people's lives. The exclusivity of this requirement thunders in no uncertain terms that anyone wanting to see God act must walk by faith. Other New Testament accounts that refer to faith as the basis for God's work include Matthew 8:13; 9:2,22,29; 15:28; 21:21; Luke 7:50; 17:19; and Acts 14:9.

"As Jesus went on from there, two blind men followed Him, shouting, 'Have mercy on us, Son of David!' When He entered the house, the blind men approached Him, and Jesus said to them, 'Do you believe that I can do this?' 'Yes, Lord,' they answered Him. Then He touched their eyes, saying, 'Let it be done for you according to your faith!' And their eyes were opened."
Matthew 9:27-30

Scripture pictures God rewarding and affirming faith, but it also shows that He does not work when faith is not present.

10. Read the verses in the margin. Name the reason Jesus refused to act in each situation.

Matthew 13:58: _____

Matthew 14:31: _____

Matthew 17:19-20: _____

Jesus refused to do miracles in His hometown because of unbelief. He pegged Peter's sinking in the water to his doubt. Jesus directly linked the disciples' inability to cast out a demon with their lack of faith. This consistent picture informs us that God's work in our lives is always tied to our faith.

This connection between God's work and our faith also applies to our prayer lives. Several New Testament verses specifically state that God requires faith for Him to answer prayer:

- "If you believe, you will receive whatever you ask for in prayer" (Matt. 21:22).
- "All the things you pray and ask for—believe that you have received them, and you will have them" (Mark 11:24).
- "If any of you lacks wisdom, he should ask God, who gives to all generously and without criticizing, and it will be given to him. But let him ask in faith without doubting. For the doubter is like the surging sea, driven and tossed by the wind. That person should not expect to receive anything from the Lord" (Jas. 1:5-7).

11. Name two or three things you have been praying for.

_____

_____

_____

"He did not do many miracles there because of their unbelief."
Matthew 13:58

"Jesus reached out His hand, caught hold of him, and said to him, 'You of little faith, why did you doubt?'"
Matthew 14:31

"The disciples ... said, 'Why couldn't we drive [the demon] out?' 'Because of your little faith,' He told them. 'For I assure you: If you have faith the size of a mustard seed, you will tell this mountain, "Move from here to there," and it will move. Nothing will be impossible for you.'"
Matthew 17:19-20

Evaluate how you've been praying in light of the bulleted verses on page 15. Have you been praying in faith?
○ Yes   ○ No

These three passages specifically state that prayer becomes effectual only when undergirded by faith. Even more commonly, we find verses reflecting that an attitude of faith is to surround prayer.

An attitude of faith is to surround prayer.

12. As you read the following verses, underline words that point to faith in prayer.

"… in whom we have boldness, access, and confidence through faith in Him" (Eph. 3:12).

"… because I know this will lead to my deliverance through your prayers and help from the Spirit of Jesus Christ. My eager expectation and hope is that I will not be ashamed about anything" (Phil. 1:19-20).

"Let us approach the throne of grace with boldness, so that we may receive mercy and find grace to help us at the proper time" (Heb. 4:16).

"The prayer of faith will save the sick person" (Jas. 5:15).

"Dear friends, if our hearts do not condemn us we have confidence before God, and can receive whatever we ask from Him" (1 John 3:21-22).

"This is the confidence we have before Him: whenever we ask anything according to His will, He hears us. And if we know that He hears whatever we ask, we know that we have what we have asked Him for" (1 John 5:14-15).

You probably underlined *faith, confidence, expectation,* and *boldness.* You can see that the spirits of the great saints were full of faith when they bowed their knees.

God obviously works in our prayer lives according to our faith. Can you think of times in Scripture when God granted requests to persons without faith? We found three examples.

1. The children of Israel continually requested water or food during their time in the wilderness. In Numbers 11 when they complained because they lacked meat, God answered that request by sending them quail to eat. But Scripture records that "while the meat was still between their teeth, before it was chewed, the LORD's anger burned against the people, and the LORD struck them with a very severe plague" (Num. 11:33).

2. Centuries later the Israelites became discontented because they had no king. They persistently asked to be "the same as all the other nations" (1 Sam. 8:5), even though God warned them that a king would tax them, draft their sons, take them for his servants, and oppress them (see 1 Sam. 8:10-17). In response God granted their request but sent a thunderstorm to show His displeasure and told them He would not deliver them when their king oppressed them (see 1 Sam. 8:18; 12:18).

3. For years Zechariah and his wife, Elizabeth, had prayed for a child. The angel Gabriel appeared to Zechariah and announced the joyful news that they would indeed have a son, even though Elizabeth was long past childbearing years. When Zechariah questioned the angel's announcement, he was struck mute until the day his son was born (see Luke 1:5-20).

13. What conclusions do you draw from these examples?
- ○ These examples highlight the fact that God works through faith.
- ○ I am afraid to ask God for anything. What if I ask wrongly?
- ○ The examples of asking for meat and a king were made by people with stubborn hearts. If I desire to do God's will but ask wrongly, He will not treat me harshly. He will redirect my prayers.
- ○ These examples show that God is serious about the requirement of faith.

Each time God granted a request when unbelief was present, He expressed His displeasure to those who asked. However, God does not sit around heaven eagerly waiting for people to violate a rule in

Each time God granted a request when unbelief was present, He expressed His displeasure to those who asked.

order to whack them over the head. You don't have to fear making a mistake in prayer if your heart desires to serve Him; nevertheless, God is very serious about the requirement of faith. These examples further highlight the fact that God works through faith.

Hudson Taylor, the famous missionary, understood that God acts in response to our faith. On his first voyage to China, his ship neared cannibal-inhabited islands as it helplessly drifted on a windless sea. The savages eagerly anticipated feasting on the hapless occupants. The captain came to young Taylor and pleaded with him to pray for God's help. "I will," Taylor said, "provided you set your sails to catch the breeze." The captain declined making himself the butt of ridicule by unfurling the sails in a calm sea. Taylor responded, "I will not undertake to pray for the vessel unless you will prepare the sails." The captain complied. Immediately, Taylor retired to his cabin and began to implore God's help. While he was still praying, the captain knocked on the door and asked, "Are you still praying for wind?" "Yes." "Well," the captain said, "you'd better stop praying, for we have more wind than we can manage."[1] Hudson Taylor knew that God worked only through faith and had rewarded him.

Jesus' teaching, the prayer lives of great New Testament saints, and examples from history all show that a connection exists between our faith and God's work in our lives.

A connection exists between our faith and God's work in our lives.

Without faith it is impossible to please God. Hebrews 11:6 rather bluntly provides further proof that God wants us to relate to Him by faith: "Without faith it is impossible to please God." *Impossible* is a shockingly intolerant word. Think about what an offensively narrow, rigid, exclusive, insensitive, discriminatory concept that word conveys. You can almost see it standing as a sergeant-at-arms at the door, battle-ax in hand, barring entrance to the legions of possibles. He emphatically tells them no. He refuses the smallest possible from even flirting with an occasional visit. No, impossible means 0 percent likelihood of ever pleasing God without faith. It cannot happen—ever.

In Hebrews 11 the list of Old Testament characters who pleased God, the intensity with which the passage was written, and the inclusion of the word *impossible* all show us whom God has affirmed throughout history. He is telling us that faith is the only way to gain His approval. It is faith or nothing at all. The 16 names of great saints and more than 15 allusions to other Bible accounts all point to one fact: the reason these people pleased God was their faith.

In fact, faith is so necessary to pleasing God that the writer of Hebrews drew conclusions about the Bible characters' faith that the Old Testament didn't spell out:

- He stated in verse 19 that Abraham assumed God was going to raise Isaac from the dead because God had promised through him to make Abraham the father of nations. Nowhere in the Old Testament is that information recorded.

- In verses 24-27 the writer gave us information about Moses that is not included in Exodus. He declared that Moses rejected the treasures of Egypt because his focus was on his reward in Christ. This means that when Moses killed the Egyptian, by faith he chose to identify with God's people in their reproach than to live in the pleasures afforded by being a member of the royal family.

- The writer of Hebrews mentioned in verse 11 that by faith Sarah received power to conceive after the time for child-bearing,[2] even though the only picture we have of Sarah prior to her pregnancy was her laughing at the tent door in unbelief. The writer knew faith was so integral to pleasing God that he concluded Sarah's heart changed within three months in order for God to grant her the power to conceive, even though Scripture doesn't record it. The writer of Hebrews could draw these conclusions because he was certain that without faith it is impossible to please God.

14. Is it possible to teach Sunday School, sing in the choir, and visit the lost but not be pleasing to God?
   ○ Yes   ○ No   **On a scale of 1 to 10, how important is it to make sure that we serve God from faith? _____**

The importance of faith as the catalyst behind our service is a 10. Therefore, faith is a prerequisite for serving God in any capacity.

Hebrews 11 provides all positive examples of those who lived by faith. Earlier in Hebrews 3 we also find a negative example that warns us about not having faith: the children of Israel did not enter the promised land because God was angry about their unbelief (see Heb. 3:17-19). This fact speaks of the seriousness of displeasing God,

"By faith Abraham, when he was tested, offered up Isaac; he who had received the promises was offering up his unique son, about whom it had been said, In Isaac your seed will be called. He considered God to be able even to raise someone from the dead, from which he also got him back as an illustration."
Hebrews 11:17-19

"You will say, 'Branches were broken off so that I might be grafted in.' True enough; they were broken off by unbelief, but you stand by faith. Do not be arrogant, but be afraid. For if God did not spare the natural branches, He will not spare you either. Therefore, consider God's kindness and severity: severity toward those who have fallen, but God's kindness toward you—if you remain in His kindness. Otherwise you too will be cut off. And even they, if they do not remain in unbelief, will be grafted in, because God has the power to graft them in again."

Romans 11:19-23

and in this case that displeasure was catastrophic. Picking up on that statement, I (John) surveyed Scripture to identify what made God most angry. I concluded that the following three sins, in particular, evoke God's displeasure.

1. *Idolatry.* The prohibition against idolatry was the First Commandment God gave of the Ten. He would have destroyed all of the children of Israel at Mount Sinai if Moses had not interceded (see Ex. 32:10-14). God killed 24,000 for serving other gods as they were about to enter the promised land (see Num. 25:9). In Judges He repeatedly turned His people over to their enemies when they served other gods. And an inconceivably horrific judgment came on Israel in 587–586 B.C. because of their idolatry (see Ezek. 5:9-13; 16:35-43).

2. *Pride.* God said the reason He destroyed Sodom and Gomorrah was because of their pride (see Ezek. 16:49). When He moved to destroy Babylon, He identified their arrogant attitude as what provoked Him most:

> *You were secure in your wickedness;*
> *you said: No one sees me.*
> *Your wisdom and knowledge*
> *led you astray.*
> *You said to yourself:*
> *I, and no one else.* ISAIAH 47:10

At the time of Moab's destruction, both Isaiah and Jeremiah listed pride as the sin (see Isa. 16:6; Jer. 48:29). The king of Assyria haughtily spoke against the Lord, so God killed 185,000 of his soldiers in one night (see Isa. 37:23,29,36).

3. *Unbelief.* When the children of Israel balked in unbelief at entering the promised land, God was ready to kill them all. Through Moses' intercession God commuted their sentence to gradual death over 40 years of wandering in the wilderness (see Num. 14:11-35). King Ahaz was warned that if he did not believe the Lord's word, he would fall (see Isa. 7:9). Unfortunately, he refused to listen, his reign was plagued by defeat in war, and he soon died at only 36 years of age. When the Jews rejected the Messiah, Paul stated that they were broken off because of unbelief and will remain so until the day they believe (see Rom. 11:19-23).

From God's perspective unbelief is very serious, ranking alongside idolatry and pride. While most believers wouldn't tolerate adultery or the use of foul language, they frequently minimize, ignore, or accept unbelief as just being human. The truth is that unbelief can have grave consequences in the life of a believer or a church.

15. Why does God view unbelief so seriously?
○ Actually, it's not that serious. God just gets irritated when people disobey Him.
○ Not responding to God delays His will and negatively affects others.
○ Unbelief calls into question God's character, power, and faithfulness.

Refusing to believe God calls into question His character, power, and faithfulness, implying that He either can't or won't come through. Not responding to God also delays the implementation of His plan and often has consequences for others. For example, when the Jewish leaders of Jesus' day did not believe, the result was that the Romans destroyed their nation. In our day the salvation of souls is affected by our obedience or disobedience. This does not mean we need to live in neurotic fear. God will be faithful to prepare our hearts and encourage us so that we respond when He speaks. In the previous examples the people exhibited a pattern of unbelief over an extended period of time after God had spoken to them on several occasions. But His judgment in these cases shows the importance of taking belief in God seriously.

16. See if you can recall the three ways we know that God desires a faith relationship with each of His children.
1. Jesus began training His disciples to _____ the moment He _____ them.
2. God _____ His work in and through your life to your _____.
3. Without _____ it is _____ to _____ God.

We know that God desires a faith relationship with us because Jesus began training His disciples to walk by faith the moment He called

> Refusing to believe God calls into question His character, power, and faithfulness, implying that He either can't or won't come through.

them, God connects His work in and through our lives to our faith, and without faith it is impossible to please Him.

Living by Faith

I (Lonnie) was once ignorant of the need to relate to God by faith, and I certainly had no practical knowledge of how to walk by faith rather than by sight. In 1991 God radically intersected my life and took it in a different direction. By all outward indications I had a successful ministry. I pastored one of the largest churches in my denomination in the state of Ohio. My church was growing, people were being saved, giving was increasing, and we had built new buildings. But in my heart I knew something was missing. At a conference that year I realized I had been serving God according to what I could accomplish with my own planning. Good things had happened, but I could explain exactly how *I* did it. My ministry was not characterized by things that only God could do.

> **17. Lonnie had a deep longing for something more than he was experiencing. Have you had similar longings?**
> ○ Yes   ○ No

After the conference I spent three days in my office weeping. Realizing how much I had failed my Lord, I asked for His forgiveness and for His help in learning how He desired a relationship with Him to work. That prayer launched a journey into living by faith that has revolutionized my life. The result is not that I've become perfect, a spiritual giant, immune to failure, smarter, or richer. Rather, I have the phenomenal joy of experiencing the presence and power of God as He does things through my life that only He can do.

The past seven years in particular have been the sweetest I have ever known. It began in 1999, when I sensed God's call to Lynch, Kentucky, in the Appalachian Mountains. This call was so clear that I resigned my church and moved there, although I had no job waiting or another means of support. All I knew was that God wanted to impact the people of that area. I determined to apply the lessons I had learned about faith. I was so fearful of reverting to my previous patterns of generating ministry by my own ingenuity that I

I have the phenomenal joy of experiencing the presence and power of God as He does things through my life that only He can do.

decided not to solicit money or call people to come help. That way I would know whatever happened would be from God.

For six months God did nothing visible, but then He opened the floodgates of heaven by establishing and working through several ministries in the region. In the particular ministry to which God has called me, more than 10,000 volunteers have come to serve on short-term mission teams. He has begun a housing ministry, a food ministry, a clothing ministry, and 11 other ministries. About $5 million in other monies, goods, and services have been contributed to these ministries. Of about 25 bars that once operated in the area, only 6 are still open. Approximately three thousand people have been converted. The area has seen a spike in its economy.

Could I have planned these blessings? Could I have developed a strategy to accomplish these results in a region where the average annual income is well below the poverty level? Absolutely not! What a transformation of joy God has wrought in my life. What a thrill to experience His presence and power accomplishing what my best efforts and planning could not have remotely touched.

We also want you to experience the joy of walking by faith. This study will teach you the scriptural pattern of how God cultivates a faith relationship with His children. The Bible teaches that a life of faith follows a five-stage process. The following five chapters in this study will address each stage, but here we will offer an overview of all five so that you will grasp the basic concept of how a lifestyle of faith functions. We will primarily use the Apostle Paul as a biblical example of the way God works and relates to believers.

Stage 1: God initiates a faith relationship. In this stage God arrests our attention and brings us into relationship with Himself. When we first meet Paul (Saul) in the Book of Acts, he had no understanding of who Jesus Christ was. He zealously persecuted Christians and even obtained permission to arrest them in faraway cities. Leaving Jerusalem, Paul journeyed on the road to Damascus when suddenly Jesus Christ radically intersected His life (see Acts 9:1-9). In this encounter God snapped Paul to attention and refocused his life onto His Son. This dramatic initiation into a relationship with God set the precedent for the rest of Paul's life. Just as Paul entered the relationship by faith, he continued living every aspect of it by faith. From his early days in Damascus, when he narrowly escaped capture (see

> God arrests our attention and brings us into relationship with Himself.

Acts 9:23-25), to his latter days in the Mediterranean storm, when he announced deliverance for all (see Acts 27:13-44), Paul lived by faith. It all began, however, at a defining moment in which God turned Paul's heart toward Him.

18. Summarize this stage by choosing the correct words or phrases below to complete the sentence.

disciplines   a defining moment   catastrophe   the heart
Bible reading   prayer   turns   church attendance   Him

In _____

God _____ our hearts toward _____.

In this initial stage God acts to begin a faith relationship with Him. In a defining moment He turns our hearts toward Him.

There is no record that Paul ever backslid in his relationship with God. However, it is possible for a Christian to turn from walking with God. Even though we are still saved, often God must radically intersect our lives all over again, as He used Nathan to reach David (see 2 Sam. 12). He must regain our attention so that we again become responsive to Him.

Stage 2: God develops fellowship for a consistent walk of faith. Once God has our attention, He begins the process of developing deeper fellowship with us so that we can consistently walk by faith. In this stage of life we must learn the habit of turning from self to God. We must learn God's character, purposes, and ways. God begins cleansing us and transforming us by His Word so that our character, our purposes, and our ways match His. Shortly after Paul was converted, he sequestered himself in Arabia for three years (see Gal. 1:17-18). What was he doing? God must have been laying the foundation Paul needed to maintain fellowship with God. When Paul went on his first missionary journeys perhaps 14 years later (see Gal. 2:1), he understood how the relationship with his Father worked. Paul did not fail because he had learned how to turn to God. Then God unveiled His will through him as Paul maintained his walk with God.

Once God has our attention, He begins the process of developing deeper fellowship with us so that we can consistently walk by faith.

19. Is this sentence true or false? Maintained fellowship with God means we've learned to walk with Him consistently by faith. ○ True ○ False

The answer is true. At this stage we understand how God works in our lives and how to respond to Him by faith. This season of life is vitally important because God does not work through us apart from the platform of maintained fellowship with Him. When we fail to walk in His love, become disobedient, or tolerate an offense we haven't made right with Him, we are in no position to walk with Him by faith. A lifestyle of faith is not a formula but a relationship. If the relationship suffers, God shuts down everything else He intends through our lives until we return to Him. Whenever we compromise our fellowship with God, we cannot walk with Him by faith.

Stage 3: God requires a faith response to the unveiling of His will. When God called Paul on the Damascus road, He also told him that he would go to the Gentiles (see Acts 9:15). Paul's faith about what God would do was *initiated* by this word of revelation from God; he didn't decide on his own to go to the Gentiles. Next Paul's faith was *enacted* when he responded to God. If he had not believed God, everything God intended to accomplish through Paul's life would have never materialized. Then Paul's faith was *visualized* when he watched to see how God would bring His word to pass. By *visualized* we mean that Paul began to see God putting pieces together:

- God revealed to Peter that His redemptive plan included the Gentiles (see Acts 10).
- The Jewish church understood this fact (see Acts 11:18).
- Persecution resulted when the gospel was preached to Gentiles in Antioch.
- Barnabas invited Paul to come to Antioch, where he spent a year. During that time God probably knit Paul's and Barnabas's hearts together and fine-tuned the message they were to preach to the Gentiles (see Acts 11:19-26).
- Paul and Barnabas served on their first traveling assignment and reported to the leaders in Jerusalem (see Acts 12:25).

Finally, God had put all of the pieces in place. Peter and the church knew that God would save Gentiles. God had trained Paul and

"The Lord said to him, 'Go! For this man is My chosen instrument to carry My name before Gentiles, kings, and the sons of Israel.'"
Acts 9:15

Barnabas and had established a home base in Antioch from which to launch their ministry. God gave them recognition with the elders in Jerusalem. Then He sent them on their journey (see Acts 13:1-3). Paul's faith was *finalized* when he responded to God's timing. He and Barnabas then saw Gentiles come to faith in Christ. This process of responding to God in faith culminated in God's unveiling His will through Paul's life.

20. Match the components of Paul's faith response with his actions.

___ 1. His faith was initiated …	a. when he watched to see how God would bring His word to pass.
___ 2. His faith was enacted …	b. when he responded to God.
___ 3. His faith was visualized …	c. by a word of revelation from God.

Check your answers: 1. c, 2. b, 3. a.

Stage 4: God matures faith through waiting. Typically, once God speaks, a waiting period follows. Paul did not go on his first missionary journey for 14 years (see Gal. 2:1). This example reflects the pattern of God's work in Scripture. Noah waited perhaps 120 years before the flood. Abraham waited 25 years before Sarah bore Isaac. Joseph waited at least 22 years before his dream came true of ruling over his family. Moses saw 40 years pass before his people were delivered from Egypt. David spent years after being anointed king before receiving the throne. Anyone who wants to walk by faith must be prepared for seasons of waiting. All waiting carries with it a test: will we take matters into our own hands, or will we wait on God? This proved to be the most difficult part of walking by faith for many biblical characters. Many who missed God missed Him at this point.

The waiting period does not imply inactivity. All of these characters were busy following God as He set things in place. The 14 years Paul waited were spent preparing and learning to handle the day when he finally began his missionary journeys. David learned leadership and developed relationships with the men who would one day administer his kingdom. Waiting means that we do not take

> Anyone who wants to walk by faith must be prepared for seasons of waiting.

into our hands what only God should do. In chapter 5 we will examine the waiting period in more detail, answering questions such as, What does waiting look like? How do I wait on God? What do I do while I wait on God?

21. Circle each statement *T* for *true* or *F* for *false*.

    T   F   1. We prove our faith by doing what we think is best.

    T   F   2. All biblical characters waited to hear from God before acting.

    T   F   3. Waiting means that we do not take into our hands what only God should do.

Statements 1 and 2 are false. We prove our faith by waiting on God, not taking matters into our own hands. Some biblical characters failed this test. Statement 3 is true.

Stage 5: God rewards completed faith. Paul finally saw God do what He said He would do. Paul became a light to the Gentiles and eventually stood before kings and the sons of Israel. He planted churches in provinces of the Roman Empire; he testified to the Sanhedrin in Jerusalem; and he spoke to governors such as Felix, Festus, and Agrippa. He was sent from Israel to Rome in an appeal to Caesar, ultimately testifying to the most powerful man on earth.

22. Describe a time when your faith became reality and you saw God act in your life.

_____

_____

When we go through the process of walking by faith, God does through us what He promised. We have the joy of His presence and the honor of being the instrument through which He does it.

Does God want to work in your life in the same way? Yes. Can you live this way? Yes. The assignment and circumstances will be different for each one of us, but God's desire for every one of His children is that we know Him. He is no respecter of persons. He does not reserve access to His presence only for the elite but makes

> When we go through the process of walking by faith, God does through us what He promised.

Himself available to anyone who is willing to walk with Him in a faith relationship. Right now God sees people on your street, in your community, in our nation, and around the globe whom He wishes to impact powerfully. Second Chronicles 16:9 states, "The eyes of the Lord range throughout the earth to show Himself strong for those whose hearts are completely His." Would you dare to be that kind of person? Would you let Him use you to stop a divorce in your church or to save a teenage girl from a destructive choice, although you have no clue how? Would you go on a mission trip to those who have never heard the good news of Jesus, even if you don't know where you'll get the money? Would you be willing to let God change your workplace or transform your neighborhood, although you've never done anything like that before? Would your heart cry out, "O Lord, may Your eyes cease scanning the earth when they fall on me! I will step out with You into the unknown in full assurance of faith. Do whatever You want through me!"?

A Walk of Faith

1. God _____ a faith relationship.

2. God develops _____ for a consistent walk of faith.

3. God requires a _____ _____ to the unveiling of His will.

4. God matures faith through _____

5. God _____ completed faith.

23. Select the statement that best describes the way you feel about walking by faith.

○ I can't walk by faith. I'm not spiritual enough.

○ I don't know how to walk by faith, but I'm willing to learn.

○ My faith is weak, but I believe God can strengthen it and use me.

○ My faith is strong, and I'm ready to follow Him to the next level.

God has equipped each of His children with the capacity to walk with Him by faith. You can do it with His help.

24. Fill in the blanks in the margin to identify the five stages in a walk of faith.

1. Paul L. Tan, *Encyclopedia of 7,700 Illustrations: Sign of the Times* (Garland, TX: Bible Communications, 1979), 1493.
2. The New International Version and some other translations say that Hebrews 11:11 refers to Abraham instead of Sarah. This discrepancy exists because the third-person singular verb in Greek is used for both masculine and feminine. The King James Version, New King James Version, New American Standard Bible, and Holman Christian Standard Bible translate the verse to refer to Sarah.

CHAPTER 2

God Initiates a Faith Relationship

God wants you to live a life of faith, but how do you do it? No doubt if you have ever channel-surfed Christian programming, you have encountered various views of what faith should look like in the Christian life. Catchphrases abound that relate to faith—*live by faith, a step of faith, trust God by faith, the gift of faith, sow in faith, name it and claim it by faith,* and many more.

Some teach that giving money in faith will ensure a tenfold return, while others call that crass materialism. Faith healers claim that God's power alone is all that's necessary for bodily cures, while others scoff, saying that God gave us doctors for a reason. Others assert that when calamity strikes, we are just to trust God, while others contend that God helps those who help themselves. Some declare the importance of faith, but they make decisions based on their circumstances or budget. Some claiming to have a word from God step out in faith and fall flat on their faces; others step out in faith, and God does a miracle.

If you are like most Christians, you wonder what following the faith examples of great biblical characters would look like—but with your head on straight. You sincerely want to follow God as completely as Abraham did; yet you do not want to act foolish. So how do you walk with God by faith? This chapter will examine the first step in that process: God initiates a faith relationship.

God Radically Intersects Our Lives

God dramatically interrupts someone's life and redirects it onto a whole new course with Him.

God initiates a faith relationship by radically intersecting someone's life. *Radical intersection* means that God dramatically interrupts someone's life and redirects it onto a whole new course with Him. This dramatic interruption is sometimes a single, spectacular encounter with God that occurs in a moment, while other times it is a brief season in a person's life. In either case God powerfully arrests the person's attention through thoughts, circumstances, an event, or other people. This interruption, this awakening, this radical intersection inducts them into a relationship characterized by faith.

> **1. Fill in the blank:**
> Radical intersection means that God dramatically _____ someone's life and redirects it onto a whole new course with Him.
>
> **Name two Bible figures whose lives God radically intersected to initiate a faith relationship.**
> 1. _____ 2. _____

God radically intersects someone's life by interrupting the person's old way of life and redirecting it into a new walk with Him. Let's look at some ways God radically intersected the lives of several biblical characters.

- On the Galilean seashore Peter, Andrew, James, and John were fishing as they did each workday. Suddenly, Jesus appeared and called them to follow Him, leaving their businesses and their homes to launch into the unknown with Him (see Matt. 4:18-22).

30

- Zacchaeus had lived a disreputable life, cheating and swindling people. When he heard that Jesus was in town, he wanted to get a glimpse as He passed by. Imagine Zacchaeus's shock when the Lord was seated in his home within the hour. Zacchaeus was so transformed by his encounter with Jesus that he gave away half his possessions to the poor and restored four times what he had stolen (see Luke 19:1-10).
- Saul zealously persecuted Christians, even in cities two hundred miles away. On the road to Damascus the Lord Jesus radically intersected Saul's life (see Acts 9:1-9). In one moment he went from an agent to extinguish the light of the gospel to a torchbearer of the good news around the world.
- The Ethiopian eunuch was returning to his country when suddenly, Philip approached his chariot. Soon God changed the eunuch from a proselytized Jew to a baptized follower of Christ (see Acts 8:26-39).
- Cornelius was a God-fearing man, constantly giving alms to the poor. One day in his prayer time an angel appeared with a message. In four short days he would have to change his declaration from "Caesar is Lord" to "Jesus is Lord" (see Acts 10:1–11:18).

> In one moment Saul went from an agent to extinguish the light of the gospel to a torchbearer of the good news around the world.

God intersected the lives of many biblical characters this way—Joseph's enslavement, Moses at the burning bush, Rahab and the two spies, Elisha called from the plow, Naaman healed of leprosy, Isaiah's catching a vision of God, Josiah's hearing the law read, Nehemiah's hearing a word about the desolation of Jerusalem, Joseph and Mary's being chosen as Jesus' earthly parents, the woman at the well, the man lame from birth, Lydia at the river's edge, and others. Whether or not they were seeking God, all of these had dramatic encounters with God that interrupted the direction of their lives.

2. Does God radically intersect lives today? ○ Yes ○ No

State the reason for your response. _____

_____

_____

God still works the same way today to bring people face-to-face with His reality. It may be something as simple as Martin Luther's choosing the ministry because of a vow made during a thunderstorm, or it may be something as tragic as Adoniram Judson's overhearing the groanings of an atheist friend who was dying an agonizing death. It may occur in difficulty, such as a failed marriage, a business demise, or a health problem. Other times a blessing may arrest someone's attention, such as the birth of a child, a promotion at work, or a sudden windfall. Sometimes it may happen in an instant; other times it may occur through a season of life. The way God works cannot be predicted, but most people can point to a specific event or season when God initiated a faith relationship with them by turning their lives in a whole new direction.

Does God always work dramatically in the life of every person He invites to walk with Him by faith?

3. Try to identify two biblical figures whose lives God intersected in a less dramatic way.

    1. _____   2. _____

It's hard to think of less dramatic examples in Scripture, isn't it? You may have named someone like Isaac or Hannah, but most examples recorded in Scripture are dramatic examples of God's intersection of lives. We would be hesitant to say that God always intersects someone's life dramatically, but if you desire to know God intimately, the chance of His doing something dramatic in your life is real. Even if you don't have a Damascus-road experience like Saul, most likely when God moves, the event will be dramatic to you. Either way, God will radically alter the whole orientation of your life to focus on Him in an intense way and to live by faith in Him.

The reason God so often acted dramatically in Scripture probably has more to do with us than Him. God used the analogy of potter and clay in several Bible passages to illustrate His work with us. We can glean many interesting spiritual insights from the properties of clay and the dynamics of the potter's efforts to shape it. One of the most fascinating is the rather odd phenomenon that clay can go to sleep. Typically, clay responds very easily and can be molded into any shape the potter wishes; however, when clay has been sedentary for an extended period of time, it becomes stiff and difficult

The reason God so often acted dramatically in Scripture probably has more to do with us than Him.

to work with. In order to make the clay malleable again, the potter must awaken it. To do this, he does not add something to or subtract anything from the clay, he mixes no water with it, and he removes no impurities; instead, He simply slams the clay on a hard surface. This jolt reactivates the properties of clay, and once again it responds to the potter's touch as readily as fresh clay.

In the same way, when our hearts are asleep, we must be awakened. Sometimes we find ourselves spiritually groggy or dozing in a comfort zone. In this state we are no more pliable to God's touch than sleeping clay is to the potter's. So God, as the Potter, must awaken us. From the clay's perspective, the hard jolt no doubt seems rather dramatic. From the potter's perspective, however, it is not theatrics but simply the means necessary to make the clay responsive. Often our sleeping hearts, like the lump of clay, must be dramatically awakened through radical intersection so that our Heavenly Potter can mold the faith relationship He desires for our lives.

> **4. True or false?** From God's perspective, the purpose of radical intersection is to make someone's heart responsive to Him. **Circle your answer:** True False

The statement is true. God's intent in intersecting our lives is to awaken us to the walk of faith He desires for us. Two kinds of sleeping hearts exist. One is actually better described as dead—a lost person who has never encountered the living God. The other kind is a Christian whom God has awakened and saved but has since gone to sleep instead of living by faith. Let's look at the way God intersects each life to walk with Him by faith.

God Radically Intersects a Lost Person's Life
We will briefly look at two occasions in the Bible when God radically intersected the lives of lost persons. One happened over a season in the life of Nicodemus. The other happened in a moment in the life of the woman at the well. In both cases we can see three dynamics at work to awaken these persons to a life of faith.

God first turns the person's attention to Himself. A lost person can go his merry way without a care about God. Have you ever heard the statement "Lost people can't be happy because something is always

God's intent in intersecting our lives is to awaken us to the walk of faith He desires for us.

33

missing in their hearts"? That sounds logical, but it's not always true. Many lost people are having the time of their lives. Quite a number have money, power, fame, and possessions. In this satisfied condition they don't plan to seek anything different. Why would they? If you were in a warm house in January with plenty of friends and food, why would you want to go out into a harsh winter night? Something must turn their attention in the direction of Jesus before they seek Him. On the other hand, many other lost people are dissatisfied, hurting, or miserable. Even in this state many can ignore God, focusing on self, medicating their misery, or choosing to live with pain because their fear of the unknown is worse than their discomfort. Many want a better life but don't know how to get it. Whatever their circumstances, whether pleasurable or painful, God must turn their attention from themselves to Him. He must awaken them through a significant event or season in their lives.

5. Read John 3:2 in the margin. What means did God use to arrest Nicodemus's attention?

_____

"Rabbi, we know that You have come from God as a teacher, for no one could perform these signs You do unless God were with him."
John 3:2

God grabbed the attention of Nicodemus, a high-ranking leader of the Jews, through Jesus' miracles. His simple statement in John 3:2 reveals just how thoroughly God had seized his interest. When telling a story, the Bible usually records only significant, bottom-line information, not full conversations. Reading the entire dialogue between Jesus and Nicodemus takes only two or three minutes. Obviously, their conversation lasted much longer than that. Therefore, the fact that Nicodemus spoke of miracles tells you the key thought of his heart, the whole reason he was there: Jesus' miracles had seized his attention.

In John 4 Jesus arrested the attention of the Samaritan woman at the well by simply talking with her. Because long-standing hatred prevented Jews and Samaritans from even speaking with each other, she asked, "How is it that You, a Jew, ask for a drink from me, a Samaritan woman?" (v. 9). As the conversation progressed, Jesus fanned her interest by speaking to her of living water. God used the woman's encounter with Jesus to draw her attention to abundant life that was available in Him.

6. Do you know a lost person whose life God has radically intersected recently? Write that person's name: _____

What does God want you to say to them to point their attention to Him?

_____

God leads the person toward a defining moment that requires a response. Nicodemus came to put a toe in the water, but Jesus immediately pulled him in over his head. Jesus ignored his comment about miracles and turned the conversation to the requirement for entering the kingdom of God: "You must be born again" (John 3:7). A confused Nicodemus wrestled to understand this statement. He then must have entered a season of life in which he moved toward Jesus. Nicodemus next appears in John 7:51, where he challenges his peers for condemning Jesus without a hearing. His final appearance occurs in John 19:39, where he helps Joseph of Arimathea prepare Jesus' crucified body for burial. By openly caring for the corpse his peers had executed, Nicodemus knowingly committed political suicide. The conversation with Jesus at night led to a defining moment for Nicodemus at the crucifixion.

The woman at the well reached her defining moment in a single conversation. Jesus led her to that moment by speaking of living water that He offered, bringing to light her questionable past and her current immoral lifestyle, then finally revealing that He was the Messiah (see John 4:7-26). His conversation led her to a defining moment in which she had to respond to Him.

> Nicodemus came to put a toe in the water, but Jesus immediately pulled him in over his head.

7. Describe the defining moment when you had to respond to God's radical intersection of your life.

_____

_____

In a defining moment God leads the person to salvation by faith. The process God used with Nicodemus and the woman at the well peaked in a moment of truth when they had to either respond to

God in faith or reject Him. Nicodemus could no longer stay in the shadows, and the woman at the well had to react to Jesus' revelation that He was the Messiah. When they responded to God in faith, He established a relationship with them. When God seeks to save someone today, He deliberately sets up circumstances in his or her life that lead to a defining moment. At that moment the person must decide whether to receive Jesus as Lord by faith.

8. When does the defining moment occur?
- ○ It happens after God has set the stage;
  then it leads to a time of decision.
- ○ It happens at the person's initiative.
- ○ It happens anytime.

The defining moment occurs when God sets the stage by arresting the person's attention and leading him or her to a point of decision. The Bible makes clear that the decision to be saved is made by faith. The Gospels sketch but do not color in the lines of salvation by faith. God reserved that privilege for a unique vessel called the Apostle Paul. Through him God gave us the Books of Romans and Galatians to explain the role of faith in salvation.

Most of the world believes we will be rewarded or punished based on our works—that if your bad outweighs your good, you will suffer punishment; if your good outweighs your bad, you will go to heaven or will be rewarded. The majority of Americans hold this belief. When asked in a Barna survey if people go to heaven because they are good, the majority said yes. God warned us through Paul that this assertion is a lie; no one will be saved because he or she is good. According to Romans 3:9-12, "Both Jews and Gentiles are all under sin, as it is written: There is no one righteous, not even one; there is no one who understands, there is no one who seeks God. All have turned away, together they have become useless; there is no one who does good, there is not even one." God also said, "All have sinned and fall short of the glory of God" (v. 23).

" 'Why do you call Me good?' Jesus asked him. 'No one is good but One—God.'"
Mark 10:18

9. Read Jesus' words in the margin. How would you defend His statement?

The vast majority of people believe they are good because they use others as their standard of comparison. But God's standard for goodness is Himself; therefore, you are good only if you have never fallen short of His glory, that is, if you have lived a sinless life as He is sinless. All of us fail by that standard. Moreover, once we become a sinner, we cannot unbecome one. Sin mastered us when it entered us at the fall (see Rom. 7:23). It controls us as its slave, and we cannot break its grip, which is evident if you've ever taken inventory of your motives or tried not to have a bad thought in a 24-hour period. Sin's motto is "Once a sinner, always a sinner."

Paul also destroyed the delusion that we can be saved by good works. He wrote in Ephesians 2:8-9, "By grace you are saved through faith, and this is not from yourselves; it is God's gift—not from works, so that no one can boast." The reason good works cannot save you is because they do not change your status as a sinner. For example, in December 2005 Tookie Williams, the cofounder of a gang and the convicted murderer of four persons, was executed for his crimes. For years prior to his execution he sought to warn others not to take the same path as he. Although he might have been sincerely sorry for what he did and might have turned others back from lives of crime, no good thing he did could alter the fact that he was a murderer. The law still required that he pay a murderer's penalty. In the same way, whatever good we do cannot alter the fact that we are sinners.

Therefore, we cannot escape God's righteous penalty for our sin. We stand in the presence of a God from whose sight no creature is hidden. Instead, all things are open and bare before the eyes of Him to whom we must give account (see Heb. 4:13). Imagine the dread horror on the day of judgment as the rags of our pretensions and the threads of our delusions are stripped away, exposing the shameful nakedness of our guilt. There we will stand before God, trembling in our stains that the pitiful efforts of self-scrubbing by good works have failed to whiten.

Yet this bleak picture, so dreadful in its finality and so unalterable by any human means, has been gloriously shattered. While we were yet without hope, God, who is rich in mercy, provided a way of His own making for us to be saved: His Son paid the penalty for our sin so that we could stand before God clothed in Jesus' righteousness. This means of salvation occurs apart from our own sickly deeds of self-righteousness. Instead, we are now saved through a

It's usually easy to find some other really bad sinner to compare ourselves to.

"I see a different law in the parts of my body, waging war against the law of my mind and taking me prisoner to the law of sin in the parts of my body."
Romans 7:23

new, living way of faith in the Son of God. As Paul wrote, "God's righteousness has been revealed … through faith in Jesus Christ, to all who believe. For we conclude that a man is justified by faith apart from works. Now to the one who works, pay is not considered as a gift, but as something owed. But to the one who does not work, but believes on Him who declares righteous the ungodly, his faith is credited for righteousness" (Rom. 3:21-22,28; 4:4-5).

10. Mark each statement *T* for *true* or *F* for *false*.

___ Salvation occurs only through faith because our works cannot earn it.

___ Salvation can be earned through works.

Salvation can occur only through faith, not works. Works would mean that you earned your salvation; God would owe it to you. Faith means you believe that God wants to give salvation to you as a gift. You cannot be saved by works because a sinner can't do anything that obligates God (except to judge him for his sin). For this reason God took the initiative to send His Son to pay the penalty for sin on the cross by dying for us. Jesus' atonement satisfied God's judgment for sin. God thoroughly and completely judged our sin in His Son; therefore, His mercy for sinners does not violate His justice.

When God offers you the gift of salvation, the one requirement He demands for you to enter a relationship with Him is that you believe Him. By faith you trust God that He has done for you what you could not do for yourself. At first glance it is foolishness to think that we do nothing to be saved except merely believe—especially in light of what great sinners we are. But at second glance it makes sense because we cannot do anything to earn God's wonderful gift of life with Him. Therefore, salvation can occur *only* by faith.

God Radically Intersects a Saved Person's Life

All lost people stand in need of God's radical intersection, but Christians can backslide and also need God to radically intersect their lives again so that they walk by faith. Due to carelessness, fear, anger, complacency, disappointment with God, or a number of other reasons, a saved person's heart can become unresponsive to God. In this condition God's intervention is required to turn the individual to Him once more. God's process for intersecting the life of a saved

By faith you trust God that He has done for you what you could not do for yourself.

person is the same as that for a lost person with one exception. He still seizes a person's attention and leads him or her to a defining moment; however, instead of leading the person into salvation by faith, He leads him or her to renew their fellowship with Him.

11. Name a biblical character whose life, though redeemed, had to be redirected toward God: _____

King David intimately knew God. He had experienced God in mighty ways when He delivered him from the lion, the bear, Goliath, the Philistines, the hand of King Saul, and the nations around him. God had granted him riches, honor, fame, power, victory, and the throne. Moreover, God had given David profound understanding into His nature, so much so that David became "a man after His own heart" (1 Sam. 13:14, NKJV). To top it off, God promised David that the Messiah would come from his family's lineage.

David handled adversity well, but power and prosperity led his heart astray. Eventually, he committed adultery and murder. God radically intersected David's life again through the prophet Nathan. In that encounter God arrested David's attention by revealing his sin and leading him to a defining moment. David's hardened heart responded in faith by becoming pliable again (see 2 Sam. 12:1-15).

Jonah is another biblical figure who knew God in ways very few did. When God instructed him to warn his enemies, the Assyrians, of looming judgment, he boarded a ship sailing in the opposite direction. God radically intersected his life through a storm and led him to a defining moment in the belly of a great fish. Jonah responded and eventually fulfilled his assignment by preaching a message of repentance to the Assyrians (see Jonah 1–3).

In the New Testament God showed Peter that He would include the Gentiles in His redemptive plan by saving a Gentile, Cornelius, right before Peter's eyes. Peter explained this truth to all of the major church leaders in Jerusalem (see Acts 10:1–11:18). However, he later gave in when certain men from James applied pressure to disassociate from Gentiles. At the moment God was launching the gospel to the whole world, Peter allowed others to influence him to oppose what God had revealed. God radically intersected his life once more, seizing his attention through a confrontation with Paul (see Gal. 2:11-14). In that defining moment Peter presumably

> David's hardened heart responded in faith by becoming pliable again.

responded by making an appropriate course correction. In each of these examples God intersected the lives of His saints to redirect them to a walk of faith with Him.

12. Describe a time when God radically intersected your life to redirect you to a walk of faith.

_____

_____

Read the Scriptures in the margin and match each reference with its message for someone whose life needs to be intersected by God.

____ 1. Psalm 51:12   a. You will be used by God
____ 2. Jeremiah 15:19   once again.
____ 3. Hebrews 12:8   b. You will rediscover the joy
     of His salvation.
     c. You will experience discipline
     until you return to God.

Remember these three scriptural truths when you find that God needs to redirect your life to a walk of faith. You may also have the opportunity to share them with other believers whose lives need radical intersection by God. Answers: 1. b, 2. a, 3. c.

What Happens When God Intersects Our Lives?

Just because God radically intersects our lives does not guarantee that we will respond correctly to Him. Jesus radically intersected the life of a rich young ruler by telling him to give away all his possessions and follow Him. The young man wanted to follow, but wanting his wealth more, he went away sorrowful (see Matt. 19:16-22). Jesus radically intersected the Pharisees' lives on many occasions. He grabbed their attention and led them to a defining moment, but when that moment came, they rejected Him. As Paul spoke before the governor Felix "about righteousness, self-control, and the judgment to come, Felix became afraid and replied, 'Leave for now, but when I find time I'll call for you'" (Acts 24:25). These and others came to their defining moments and turned away. Others came to that moment and began by following God but didn't persevere. God warned Balaam by making a donkey speak, but his greed eventually overcame his initial obedience (see Num. 22:28-34; 25:1-9; 31:16). God's Spirit empowered Samson, but he never learned the self-discipline to reject immoral relationships with women (see Judg. 14:2; 16:1,4) and was eventually disqualified from leadership.

Clay must have certain properties for the potter to mold it. To be spiritually pliable in your relationship with God, you must have three properties when God radically intersects your life.

Focus on God instead of self. If we are lost, backslidden, or spiritually immature, we think very little of God. We make our decisions according to what pleases us. We conform everything in our lives to our personal preferences. But when God radically intersects our lives, we suddenly have a new blip on our radar screen. We begin to think about God. When we make decisions, we begin to ask ourselves questions such as, *What does God think of this? Does He have a plan for my life? What is He doing in this circumstance?*

In Genesis 25 and 27 Jacob opportunistically acquired his brother Esau's birthright and then stole his blessing. Esau, seething with rage, swore to kill Jacob, who fled for his life to the faraway city of Haran. Along the way he stopped in Bethel. That night God appeared to him in a dream and announced that He would provide for him, bring him home safely, and give him the promised land. Jacob vowed that if God granted provision and safety, then the Lord would indeed be his God. Jacob suddenly perceived God's hand at work in his life, and from that moment on he was awakened to his relationship with God. God's radical intersection began the process of moving Jacob from self-centeredness to God-centeredness.

> Clay must have certain properties for the potter to mold it.

13. If God has radically intersected your life, has it resulted in your viewing life from His perspective? On a scale of 1 to 10, how much of your everyday life is God-centered?

1   2   3   4   5   6   7   8   9   10

Human-centered   God-centered

Surrender your desires to God's desires. For your relationship with God to take shape in His hands, you must have a growing hunger to do His will. You can't focus on God without realizing that His desires don't always match yours. At some point conflict will arise, and you must decide whose will to follow—yours or God's. That's why Jesus explicitly stated, "If anyone wants to come with Me, he must deny himself, take up his cross daily, and follow Me" (Luke 9:23). To deny self means to reject your personal choices, decisions, habits, desires, comforts, and preferences if they conflict with God's will. An altar of sacrifice will appear, and it will cost you.

Anyone who preaches a relationship with God devoid of a price deceives his listeners. Abraham had to leave his home, Moses had to risk his life to confront Pharaoh, Daniel endured a lions' den, and the disciples left their jobs. Ultimately, God always gives a greater reward than the sacrifice required, but it doesn't come until later. We must always pay a price on the front end. Abraham became known as the father of faith only after leaving his hometown, Ur (see Rom. 4:9-12). Moses' receiving the law at Sinai followed enduring Pharaoh's anger. Daniel's promotion to third in the kingdom came after the lions' den. Jesus' resurrection was preceded by the cross. All of the suffering is temporary and all of the rewards eternal. Make no mistake, the price pales in comparison to the reward. As Paul said, "Our momentary light affliction is producing for us an absolutely incomparable eternal weight of glory" (2 Cor. 4:17). However, the person who does not expect to pay a price may be disillusioned.

Many believers' budding faith relationship becomes diseased at this point because they fail to put God's desires ahead of their own. Consider the life of King Saul. God radically intersected his life when Samuel, the prophet, found him and anointed him king. But instead of meditating on what God wanted, Saul let his fear of the position overwhelm him. This fear so conquered him that on the day he was to be revealed to the nation as king, he hid himself among the supplies (see 1 Sam. 10:22). This failure to focus on God's desires more than his own plagued him throughout his ministry and short-circuited the faith God sought to develop in him. Ultimately, it led to his removal as king.

At some point conflict will arise, and you must decide whose will to follow—yours or God's.

14. Is there anything in your life that threatens your obedience to God? ○ Yes ○ No

If so, ask God for grace to surrender it so that it will not rob you of what He intends for you.

In contrast to Saul, others made the transition to a life of faith by surrendering their will to God's. In John 9 Jesus radically intersected the life of a man born blind from birth by healing him on the Sabbath. Infuriated, the Pharisees belligerently questioned the man and ultimately threatened him. As the story unfolds, you can see that the man's focus on God and his desire to do His will were leading him toward a faith relationship with Jesus. At the start of the questioning, we learn that the man knew so little about Jesus that he had no idea where He was (see v. 12). When asked by the arguing Pharisees who the man thought Jesus was, he ventured a step in Jesus' direction by replying, "He is a prophet" (v. 17).

In the next round of questioning, his parents wouldn't support the man, and the Pharisees intensified their pressure. They tried to manipulate his testimony by declaring that Jesus was a sinner and lacked credibility because they didn't know where He was from. Steeled by a rising tide of understanding, the besieged man stepped into the waters of no return: "Now that's amazing! Why in the world can't you figure out where He's from? Never before in the history of the world has anybody ever opened the eyes of someone born blind. God doesn't listen to sinners, so what does that tell you about this man? If He weren't from God, He couldn't do anything!" (vv. 30-33, authors' paraphrase). In response the Pharisees threw him out, but Jesus found him. When He revealed Himself as the Messiah, the man quickly took the final step of entering a faith relationship by declaring, "I believe, Lord!" (v. 38). The man's increasing desire to please God required a sacrifice, but he received a relationship with God and the honor of being recorded in Scripture as an example.

As we grow in our relationship with God and practice walking by faith, He will lead us to a time when the desire to do His will becomes stronger than the desire to do our will. That reward then serves to further increase our faith.

As we grow in our relationship with God and practice walking by faith, He will lead us to a time when the desire to do His will becomes stronger than the desire to do our will.

Become teachable. Typically, when God began leading people in Scripture, He led them into the unknown. He required changes in their belief system, habits, role, or character. Most received assignments they could never live up to on their own. Do you think Moses had any inkling what lay before him when God called him at the burning bush? He would become a deliverer, an administrator, an intercessor, a lawgiver, and a nation builder. He went from doubt about his speaking abilities at the burning bush to trusting God to split the Red Sea. God began to transform him as he trusted Him by faith with a teachable spirit. The unknown requires that we continue relying on God throughout the process with that same teachable spirit.

Interestingly, God did not grant skills or great faith to Moses at his call. God gave these attributes to Moses as he obeyed. Moses didn't wait until he was qualified; rather, God qualified him in the process of his obedience. Teachability is an attitude that rejects the clamoring voices of fear insisting that we return to our comfort zone. Moses mastered this ability, willingly ignoring his fears of incompetence and trusting God to make him competent. Because of his teachable spirit, God enabled him to do things he never dreamed possible. The same is true today of those who remain teachable as they walk by faith.

> Teachability is an attitude that rejects the clamoring voices of fear insisting that we return to our comfort zone.

15. Check the statement that best reflects your feelings about allowing God to teach you how to walk by faith.

○ I assume that God will lead me out of a comfort zone. I'm not intimidated by my lack of experience; I know He can teach me to meet the requirements of His assignment for me.

○ You mean a relationship with God always requires change?

○ I'll be happy to trust God, but I don't think it will mean any significant changes.

○ Other: _____

God-centeredness, surrender to God's desires, and teachability position us to experience God in a faith relationship. To persevere in our walk with God, we must always keep in mind a fundamental understanding: when God radically intersects our lives, He begins teaching us that faith is relational in nature.

Faith Is Relational in Nature

Have you ever watched an interstate being built? An army of heavy machinery assaults the earth. Bulldozers, diggers, earthmovers, dump trucks, packers, and graders swarm over the future roadbed as they force proud mountains and slimy swamps into submission. Next they skillfully layer the emerging highway with gravel, rebar, and concrete before they crown it with smooth blacktop. Isn't it interesting that for all their months of labor, asphalt is the only part of their work that can be seen? But which proves more vital to the success of the road—the seen or the unseen?

When we study the spiritual giants in the Bible, it's easy to see the asphalt of their lives. Noah built an ark, Abraham laid Isaac on the altar, Elijah called down fire from heaven, and Mary submitted to the angel's announcement. However, have you ever wondered what kind of foundation lay beneath those great acts of faith? What caused them to readily respond to God in obedience?

God had prepared the lives of these saints with one foundation in particular. In the Gospels we can almost see an Under Construction sign over the lives of the disciples as Jesus dug out the obstacles and scraped away the rubble. Watch how Jesus built their understanding of the nature of faith.

16. Read the verses in the margins on this page and page 46. Underline the cure for the disciples' "little faith."

Each Scripture connects faith to the person of God. When Jesus rebuked the sea, the disciples were in awe of Him. When He admonished against worrying about clothing, it was because God would provide for them. When Jesus rescued Peter from the waves, they said, "Truly You are the Son of God!" (Matt. 14:33).

Jesus did not want the disciples to have faith in something but in Someone. He wanted them to trust *Him,* to respond to *Him,* to look to *Him.* He didn't encourage them to have faith that the storm would stop; He wanted them to have faith that *He* could stop the storm. He didn't want them to have faith that they would have clothing; He wanted them to have faith that *God* would clothe them. He didn't want Peter to have enough faith to walk on water; He wanted him to have faith in the *One* who invited him to walk on water. God

"If that's how God clothes the grass of the field, which is here today and thrown into the furnace tomorrow, won't He do much more for you— you of little faith?"
Matthew 6:30

"He said to them, 'Why are you fearful, you of little faith?' Then He got up and rebuked the winds and the sea. And there was a great calm. The men were amazed and asked, 'What kind of man is this?—even the winds and the sea obey Him!'"
Matthew 8:26-27

"Immediately Jesus reached out His hand, caught hold of him, and said to him, 'You of little faith, why did you doubt?' When they got into the boat, the wind ceased. Then those in the boat worshiped Him and said, 'Truly You are the Son of God!'"

Matthew 14:31-33

does not want to build faith in your life but faith in Him. He wants you to respond to a Person, not a concept. You don't try to work up a belief but to deepen a relationship. You don't try to have enough faith to see miracles or great exploits; you trust a Person. Before God can pave your life with asphalt, He must first lay the proper road-bed. You can't be a Hebrews 11 Christian without understanding this concrete-and-rebar truth: faith is relational in nature.

Often it's hard for Christians to live with a relational sense of faith. Too often we concentrate on what we believe about Jesus rather than believing Jesus. One reason is that we misunderstand what faith is. The Bible has at least three primary definitions of *faith*.

1. Faith is the set of truths, beliefs, and doctrines that make up a religion. For example, after resolving church conflict over the care of widows, Luke recorded in Acts 6:7, "The preaching about God flourished, the number of the disciples in Jerusalem multiplied greatly, and a large group of priests became obedient to the faith." We use *faith* in this sense when we speak of the Christian faith, the Hindu faith, the Moslem faith, and so on. This usage occasion-ally occurs in the New Testament after the Gospels.

2. Faith is the mode by which we receive salvation. For example, the Apostle Paul wrote in Romans 5:1-2, "Since we have been declared righteous by faith, we have peace with God through our Lord Jesus Christ. Also through Him, we have obtained access by faith into this grace in which we stand, and we rejoice in the hope of the glory of God." Similarly, he explained in Galatians 3:23, "Before this faith came, we were confined under the law, impris-oned until the coming faith was revealed." This definition of *faith* refers to the way we enter the new covenant with God. Its usage is common after Acts, especially in Paul's writings.

3. Faith is the trust, confidence, or expectation we have in God. Examples of this usage include Jesus' expression "You of little faith" (Matt. 6:30), Paul's statement "We walk by faith, not by sight" (2 Cor. 5:7), and the phrase *by faith* in Hebrews 11. This confidence in God sometimes refers to a single encounter with the Lord. At other times it refers to a lifestyle of habitually respond-ing to God in this manner. The majority of times the word *faith* appears in the Bible, it has this meaning. In fact, this usage occurs more than the other two meanings combined.

17. Read the verses in the margin. Match each definition of *faith* with the Scripture that illustrates its meaning.

___ 1. The set of Christian beliefs   a. Matthew 15:28
___ 2. The mode of salvation   b. Ephesians 2:8
___ 3. Our trust in God   c. Acts 14:21-22

The answers are 1. c, 2. b, 3. a. Did you catch an important distinction among these definitions? See if you can identify it in this exercise.

18. Write *T* for *true* or *F* for *false* in each blank. The third definition of *faith* (trust in God) is different from the other two because it—

___ addresses what your mind believes rather than how your heart responds;

___ deals with how you interact with God instead of just your belief about God's truth;

___ requires that you relate to God instead of just believe certain concepts about Him;

___ does not demand action from you, only right belief about doctrine.

The correct answers are *F, T, T, F*. Whereas definitions 1 and 2 primarily use *faith* in a conceptual sense, the third definition uses it in a relational sense. The first two address a religious belief system and the mode for being saved. The last one addresses how people interact with and respond to God after salvation. When Paul said, "We walk by faith" (2 Cor. 5:7), he was not referring to his conversion or a creed but his lifestyle of trusting in God. He had in mind going on missionary journeys, enduring prison with joy, depending on God for provision, and receiving God's direction and power. His relationship with God was characterized by trust, confidence, and expectation in Him and was expressed in a lifestyle of action.

A towering implication arises from this truth like a giant redwood: believing the right things about God without responding to Him is not faith. You can't have a relationship with someone you've only studied about. God does not desire orthodoxy (believing the right doctrine) devoid of orthopraxy (responding to God the right way). If you know every verse in the Bible but don't know how to relate to God in your everyday life, what good is your knowledge?

"Jesus replied to her, 'Woman, your faith is great. Let it be done for you as you want.' And from that moment her daughter was cured."
Matthew 15:28

"By grace you are saved through faith."
Ephesians 2:8

"After they had evangelized that town and made many disciples, they returned to Lystra, to Iconium, and to Antioch, strengthening the hearts of the disciples by encouraging them to continue in the faith."
Acts 14:21-22

Faith is not about *what* you believe as much as *whom* you believe.

You must interact with Him. You must relate to Him. You cannot believe only a set of facts. To have a genuine walk of faith, you have to respond to a Person. Faith is not about *what* you believe as much as *whom* you believe. Conversely, if you doubt, you don't doubt a fact; you doubt *God*. You don't have trouble believing; you have trouble believing *God*. You don't fail to believe; you fail to believe *God*.

That's why the faith of biblical characters was defined by the way they related to God. Consider a few saints listed in Hebrews 11. Did Abraham merely sit around Ur quoting verses, or did he get up and move when God spoke (see v. 8)? Did Moses content himself with meditating on God, or did he obey by forsaking the riches of Egypt to cast his lot with the Hebrews (see vv. 24-26)? Did Joshua just sing great songs about God, or did he march around Jericho (see v. 30)? Did Rahab just talk about God's greatness, or did she hide the spies and then send them on their way (see v. 31)? How many biblical characters limited their beliefs about God to a bland propositional truth instead of trusting Him in a faith relationship?

Unfortunately, many books on faith and many churches limit their discussion of faith to the first two definitions and ignore the primary definition the Bible uses. As a result, many believers know *what* to believe about God, but they don't know *how* to believe God. They know biblical concepts, but they don't know how to respond to a Person in faith.

> **19. What has your experience been? Write the percentages indicating the amount of teaching you have received on each meaning of the word *faith*.**
> Definition 1: faith as beliefs about God:
> ____ percent of your training
> Definition 2: faith as the mode by which we are saved:
> ____ percent of your training
> Definition 3: faith as walking in a relationship of confidence and trust in God: ____ percent of your training

Please understand that the first two definitions represent valid, biblical meanings of *faith*. But we must recognize that the third definition has been largely ignored, resulting in a lack of understanding about how to walk day by day in a faith relationship with God. We hope that this study will help you learn to do that.

Knowing how to relate to God in faith would have spared me (John) a great trial as a young man. Having grown up in a wonderful minister's home and having been active in church, its programs, and many Bible studies, I had acquired an orthodox belief system. Yet when I was a freshman in college, a fledgling doubt conceived and gave birth to a full-grown monster that pursued me for six years. "Am I really saved?" came to be the question I awoke with in the morning, the question I dwelled on throughout the day, and the last thing on my mind at bedtime.

I went to seminary solely to settle this question. While there I tried fasting, counseling, and a rigid discipline of Bible study and prayer to get an answer. None of this helped; however, a turnaround came when I read that Martin Luther and John Wesley had similar experiences. Even though nothing had changed, I concluded that God would bring me through this period of doubt as well. At that moment I made the most pivotal decision of my life: I would no longer wait to serve God until I had settled the question. Instead, by faith I would serve Him in the midst of my fear, trusting that He would eventually deliver me. About 20 months later He delivered me in a dramatic way. God became real when I stopped trying to make sure my faith was sincere enough and started obeying Him regardless of my fears. To my great shock, my deliverance had not waited on my belief system *about* God but on my response system *to* God.

> By faith I would serve Him in the midst of my fear, trusting that He would eventually deliver me.

20. Take an inventory of your relationship with God. Check each statement that is true of you.
- ○ I know how to approach God as a Person.
- ○ My prayer time is a joy. I really sense a relationship with God.
- ○ I hear God's voice well enough to know how to receive encouragement from Him.
- ○ I have enough history with God to trust Him when He calls me to a difficult assignment.
- ○ When I am afraid, I know how to receive strength from God.

Beside the items you checked, place an up arrow if you are growing in that area or a down arrow if you are not.

Does Faith Mean We Can Name It and Claim It?

Understanding that faith is relational in nature equips us to evaluate a popular teaching called Word of Faith. Proponents of this position teach the following.

1. God promises to grant whatever we ask for in faith (see Matt. 21:22; Mark 11:23-24; John 14:12-14).
2. If you truly pray in faith, you will always receive what you ask for. Your word of faith has power; you can name and claim whatever you want.
3. If you do not receive what you asked for, it's because you don't have enough faith.

The first Word of Faith teaching is indeed biblical. However, the last two assertions depart from biblical teaching in the following ways.

All of Jesus' promises and teachings on prayer assume that the request seeks to further God's kingdom, not personal desires. Jesus specifically taught His disciples not to pray in the heathen mode (see Matt. 6:7), which was to badger God about personal needs and desires. Rather, He commanded us to pray in the kingdom mode:

> *Your kingdom come.*
> *Your will be done*
> *on earth as it is in heaven.* MATTHEW 6:10

In Jesus' teachings in the margin, Jesus was not saying that if we want a pink Cadillac, all we need to do is work up enough faith for God to give it to us. Instead, He was teaching that we can ask for and receive whatever is needed to fulfill God's will. If a pink Cadillac is necessary for God's will to be done, then you can pray for it in faith with absolute confidence. If it's just something you really want, don't expect God to grant your request (see Jas. 4:3).

All of the biblical promises about praying in faith assume that God sets the agenda, not that a person creates a wish list. In John 14:12-14 Jesus' promise to do anything we ask in His name is connected to the condition that we do the works He did. Jesus'

"If you believe, you will receive whatever you ask for in prayer."
Matthew 21:22

"The one who believes in Me will also do the works that I do. And he will do even greater works than these, because I am going to the Father. Whatever you ask in My name, I will do it so that the Father may be glorified in the Son. If you ask Me anything in My name, I will do it."
John 14:12-14

works did not stem from His own initiative but from whatever He saw His Father do (see John 5:19). If Jesus has initiated the work, you can pray with complete confidence. If He has not, then it doesn't matter how much faith you have; your request will not be granted.

Faith must not be placed in faith but only in God. Remember that faith is relational in nature. We trust a Person, not how much faith we have manufactured or a word of faith that we speak. When the Apostle Paul pleaded three times for His thorn to be removed, God's answer was no. Obviously, Paul did not lack the faith that God could do it. Instead, when God told him He had a greater reason for the thorn, Paul believed Him (see 2 Cor. 12:7-10). He focused on trusting a Person, not trying to believe for a certain outcome. God was the object of his faith, not his desire to have the thorn removed.

> *"You ask and don't receive because you ask wrongly, so that you may spend it on your desires for pleasure."*
> James 4:3

> *"I assure you: The Son is not able to do anything on His own, but only what He sees the Father doing. For whatever the Father does, the Son also does these things in the same way."*
> John 5:19

21. Circle whether the following statements are *WF* (Word of Faith–name it and claim it) or *BF* (biblical faith).

WF BF I'm tired of being poor. I'm sowing some seed money of faith, knowing that God will give me a tenfold return to buy a house.

WF BF God led me to start a new ministry, although I have no money. Because He started it, I know He will provide.

WF BF A family member is sick. I am claiming his healing.

WF BF One of my family members is sick. Today when I was praying, God told me He would heal her. I believe Him.

Is your faith based on what God told you, or is it your own idea? Is the object of your faith God or your own word of faith? The answers to the activity are *WF, BF, WF,* and *BF.* In 1945 my (John's) grandmother was diagnosed with bladder cancer, and the doctors gave her from six months to two years to live. The news couldn't have come at a worse time for my grandfather. God had called him into the ministry about a year earlier, and he had begun making major life changes in his late 30s, including selling his business and enrolling in college. Most important of all, their three children needed their mother. On hearing the news, my grandfather went into the woods to pray. He came back with a word from God that He would heal my

A Walk of Faith

1. _____
   _____
   _____ .

2. God develops fellowship for a consistent walk of faith.

3. God requires a faith response to the unveiling of His will.

4. God matures faith through waiting.

5. God rewards completed faith.

grandmother; therefore, he continued with his education. God did just that, and she lived to the age of 86.

God does not always make His will plain in every instance like this, but when He does, we can believe Him. The keys are to place our faith in God rather than in our own faith and to position ourselves to hear a word of truth from Him instead of mustering a word of faith that originates from our personal desires. In the next chapter we will learn how to position ourselves to hear God so that we can develop a lifestyle of walking with Him by faith.

22. In the margin write the first stage in a walk of faith. Read the other stages you will study in the coming chapters.

This chapter described the way God initiates a faith relationship with us by radically intersecting our lives. The purpose of this radical intersection is to make our hearts pliable in responding to Him. Our hearts become pliable and useful to God when we focus on Him instead of ourselves, surrender our desires to His, and become teachable. When we understand that faith is relational in nature, we learn to place our trust, confidence, and expectation in God. Ultimately, true faith is grounded in believing a Person, not an outcome.

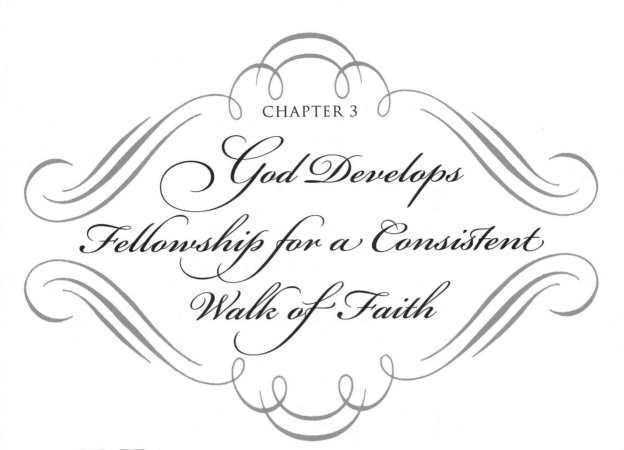

CHAPTER 3

God Develops Fellowship for a Consistent Walk of Faith

Have you ever noticed that many great biblical characters seem to magically appear in Scripture? Noah, for example, has no introduction in the Bible. We know nothing about his childhood, how he found his wife, or what he did the first few hundred years of his life. Instead, the Bible simply starts with God's call for him to build the ark. Similarly, silence cloaks the first decades of Abraham's life. His childhood, his joys, his pains, the lessons he learned—everything about him remains veiled to our eyes until his 75th year.

No doubt, Joshua served an important leadership role for Israel, but we don't know he exists until Exodus 17:9, when Moses charges him to fight the Amalekites. Gideon's first mention occurs at his call to be a deliverer. Elijah shows up in Scripture without even a single sentence of introduction.

For others—like Jacob, Joseph, Samuel, David, Daniel, John the Baptist, and Jesus—the Bible gives only a precious snippet of their births or youths. In some cases the Bible omits information about their early years; in others it records only the bare facts. Wouldn't you like to know about their childhoods? What was God doing with them in their youths to prepare them for service? How did He teach them the kind of faith required to be an ark builder, a father of nations, a military hero, or a prophet?

1. What do you think God was doing in the lives of these biblical figures during their early years?

○ I don't know.

○ I think God was training them. He was developing the understanding and habits they needed to walk with Him by faith.

○ I don't think it matters. If it did, God would have told us.

○ Other: _____

At a minimum we know that God was training these key figures to walk with Him by faith. Except for a few verses, we don't see their training, just as people today don't normally observe an orchestra's practice sessions or a football team's training camps. But we know what God was doing in these cases. We have to train for the performance we want. What we practice determines the way we perform. Therefore, we know what God did to prepare these spiritual giants by observing the way they walked with Him when they appeared on the grand stage of Scripture.

God Trains Us to Walk in Fellowship with Him

After God radically intersects someone's life to initiate a faith relationship, He begins to systematically and thoroughly develop the understanding and habits needed to walk with Him by faith. He does this by teaching us to maintain fellowship with Him, that is, to keep our relationship with Him in good standing. Deep, abiding, current fellowship with God is required to walk by faith consistently.

By peeking into the window of David's early life, we can see God's development of his fellowship with Him. In 1 Samuel 16:13 God radically intersected his life when Samuel anointed him king.

"Samuel took the horn of oil, anointed him in the presence of his brothers, and the Spirit of the LORD took control of David from that day forward."
1 Samuel 16:13

54

From "that day forward" the Spirit of God came on David to train him to walk in fellowship with God. When David volunteered to fight Goliath, Saul tried to discourage him because of his youth. David pleaded his case before Saul by relating the times he had killed a lion and a bear while tending sheep: "The LORD who rescued me from the paw of the lion and the paw of the bear will rescue me from the hand of this Philistine" (1 Sam. 17:37). God's Spirit had been teaching David in his youth to trust God by putting him in impossible, life-threatening situations. When Goliath boasted, the hapless man had the grave misfortune of an ill-timed mouth (see 1 Sam. 17:43-44). The physical giant met a spiritual one in David, who had learned how to maintain active fellowship with God. Outwardly, both armies thought little David stood no chance, but in reality it was poor Goliath who never had a prayer.

> God's Spirit had been teaching David in his youth to trust God by putting him in impossible, life-threatening situations.

2. Reflect on ways God has trained you to maintain fellowship with Him. List two lessons you have learned.

1. _____

2. _____

God also worked through Joseph's trials to teach him how to walk in fellowship with God. When Joseph's brothers sold him into slavery, he was thrown into prison in Egypt by his master, Potiphar, "an officer of Pharaoh and the captain of the guard" (Gen. 39:1), on the false charge of attempted rape. However, through God's miraculous intervention years later, Pharaoh took Joseph from prison and made him second in command over Egypt (see 41:40-41).

As a high official in Pharaoh's court, Joseph undoubtedly had regular contact with Pharaoh's officers. Can you imagine how Potiphar, the one who had unjustly condemned Joseph to prison, must have sweated and squirmed? He must have tossed and turned in terror after his former slave became his master. Opportunity had set before Joseph the table of every delectable vengeance imaginable, but the Spirit of God was training him to forgive in preparation for an even greater assignment nine years later. When Joseph's brothers appeared at that time, his fellowship with God enabled him to forgive them for betraying him into slavery (see 45:5-8).

The Gospels record the disciples' training to walk in fellowship with God. Jesus constantly pressed them to practice faith, to demonstrate humility toward one another, and to learn God's ways. They often faltered while learning their lessons, but they had so mastered them by the time of the Book of Acts that they became instruments in God's hands to turn the Roman world upside down (see Acts 17:6).

These scriptural examples depict the pattern God uses to develop in us a consistent faith walk with Him.

3. From the biblical examples you have read, why do you think this stage in your walk with God is so important?

_____

_____

_____

_____

_____

> God has tied everything about our lives—our intimacy with Him, our blessings, our rewards, and our usefulness to Him—to our ability to walk by faith.

This stage of our faith walk is incredibly important because God has tied everything about our lives—our intimacy with Him, our blessings, our rewards, and our usefulness to Him—to our ability to walk by faith. Therefore, after God radically intersects our lives, He begins teaching us how to maintain fellowship with Him. What David, Joseph, and the disciples learned in spiritual boot camp about walking in fellowship with God equipped them with faith to fulfill later assignments on the battlefield of life. They learned His character, His purposes, and His ways. They learned to recognize Him at work in their lives and to respond to Him immediately. They learned to focus on God, to identify His leading, to trust Him, and to deny self. When their fellowship with Him had become consistent, they were in a position to respond to God in faith. When we learn to walk by faith as these did, we are also in a position to receive God's guidance and to know His will.

God Guides Us Only Through Maintained Fellowship with Him

If the biblical saints had obeyed God one day but not the next, they would have been too unreliable for God to use. In the same way, God can guide us only when our fellowship with Him is current. Two implications follow.

You are not in position to live by faith unless you maintain fellowship with God. You must maintain fellowship with God to walk by faith. If you have never spent the time and energy necessary to learn how to relate to God, you will be unable to walk with Him by faith. This only makes logical sense. If you cannot recognize His guidance, what is the likelihood that you'll understand how He wants to use you? God might want to work through you to teach teenage boys how to become men, but you would miss His leading. He might have in mind reaching an ethnic group through an opportunity He lays before you, but you would never know it. He might want you to minister to women in abusive relationships, but you would be oblivious to His desire.

If you learned to walk with God in the past but have fallen out of fellowship with Him, you cannot respond appropriately to His will. If David had been out of fellowship with God, He might have shrunk back from Goliath, thus allowing a whole army to be defeated. Joseph might have repaid his brothers by selling them into slavery instead of forgiving them and thus preserving the lineage of the Messiah. The disciples might have returned to fishing on the Sea of Galilee instead of being instruments through which the early church was established. If you have not persevered in the lessons God has taught you, you cannot expect Him to give you a faith assignment until you reestablish the practices He has already taught you.

When you have developed this kind of fellowship with God, you are in the flow of everything He wants to do in and through your life. You are positioned to receive His blessings, His guidance, His assignments, and everything else He desires for you. Look at the diagram on page 58. The outer borders represent the boundaries God set for fellowship with Him. God's blessings flow to us within the parameters of that fellowship. If we step out of fellowship with God, we step out of the flow of His work in our lives.

When you have developed this kind of fellowship with God, you are in the flow of everything He wants to do in and through your life.

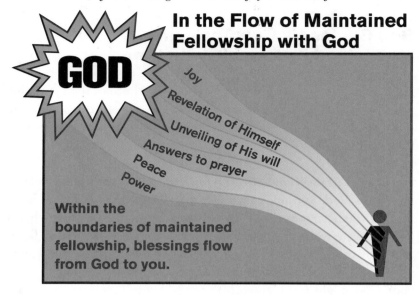

In the Flow of Maintained Fellowship with God

GOD

Joy
Revelation of Himself
Unveiling of His will
Answers to prayer
Peace
Power

Within the boundaries of maintained fellowship, blessings flow from God to you.

4. Check the things that happen when you don't maintain your fellowship with God.
○ You miss plans God has for you.
○ It becomes easier to hear God's voice.
○ You receive God's blessings.
○ God reveals His will to you.

> *"I will ask the Father, and He will give you another Counselor to be with you forever. The Counselor, the Holy Spirit—the Father will send Him in My name— will teach you all things and remind you of everything I have told you."*
> John 14:16,26

Only the first statement should be checked. Only when you maintain your fellowship with God can you discern His plans, hear His voice, receive His blessings, and know His will.

You cannot settle for part-time fellowship with God. The truth that God guides us only through maintained fellowship has a second implication: God wants to have consistently dynamic fellowship, not part-time fellowship, with us. Faith is full-time fellowship with God. He sent His Holy Spirit to ensure that we experience ongoing, growing fellowship with the Father (see John 14:16,26).

If your mind has a pause button, this would be a good time to punch it. Taking a five-minute break to write the following fact 10 times or to tape it to your bathroom mirror wouldn't be out of order. Everything that follows in this book depends on grasping this truth: we cannot have part-time fellowship with God. We cannot consistently mishandle our relationship with God and expect to walk with Him by faith.

The Book of Acts records that a Samaritan sorcerer named Simon believed in Jesus. "After he was baptized, he went around constantly with Philip and was astounded as he observed the signs and great miracles that were being performed" (Acts 8:13). Some time later Peter and John arrived from Jerusalem and began laying their hands on the new Samaritan believers, praying that they would receive the Holy Spirit. When Simon saw that the Holy Spirit came on those the apostles laid their hands on, he wanted to buy the power to do the same thing. Peter rebuked him: "You have no part or share in this matter, because your heart is not right before God" (v. 21).

Simon wanted to do something of a spiritual nature; he even had faith that God could give him that power through the apostles. But Peter forcefully told him that his fellowship with God was not right; therefore, he could not expect God to do anything through him. From Simon's experience we see that walking by faith requires that our fellowship with God remain in good standing.

Have you ever known anyone who had a position in the church, maybe a minister, a deacon, or a Sunday School teacher, and wanted to lead people spiritually but tolerated sin in his or her life? Perhaps this person had a problem with anger, was involved in an affair, or didn't love others.

5. What is the likelihood that this person could boldly step out in faith for God's use?

○ Unlikely until he or she makes things right with God

○ Impossible until he or she makes things right with God

○ A good possibility

Numerous Bible passages support the fact that God does not use those who are out of fellowship with Him.

Not surprisingly, God's response to us in our times of need also depends on maintaining fellowship with Him. We cannot ignore or take for granted our relationship with God and then expect Him to jump when we snap our fingers. Scripture records that the Israelites repeatedly did evil in God's sight, so He turned them over to their enemies for 18 years. When they finally cried out to the Lord for deliverance, God responded, "When the Egyptians, Amorites, Ammonites, Philistines, Sidonians, Amalekites, and Maonites oppressed you, and you cried out to Me, did I not deliver you from

We cannot ignore or take for granted our relationship with God and then expect Him to jump when we snap our fingers.

their power? But you have abandoned Me and worshiped other gods. Therefore, I will not deliver you again. Go and cry out to the gods you have chosen. Let them deliver you in the time of your oppression" (Judg. 10:11-14). God let the Israelites know that they couldn't presume on His grace. They couldn't be casual about their relationship with Him and then expect Him to come running when they were in trouble. God refused to help them until the respect necessary for proper fellowship with God had been reestablished. When the severity of God's answer and the misery of their affliction had corrected their careless hearts, He delivered them (see vv. 15-16).

Have you ever known people who gave God only an occasional nod, then got in a crisis and suddenly wanted His help? Perhaps they had mismanaged their finances and now faced bankruptcy; had so damaged their marriages that divorce papers had been served; had been fired for laziness; or had harshly treated their children, who were now rebelling. Then they cried out to God for help, but He did not seem to pay attention. Did their friends or church leaders explain to them that God would not respond until they made things right with Him? Believers must understand that we cannot have part-time fellowship with God if we are to walk by faith.

> We cannot have part-time fellowship with God if we are to walk by faith.

6. Do you know of someone presently in a similar situation?
◯ Yes   ◯ No

How can you pray for that person? _____

_____

What does God want you to say or do to guide this person into closer fellowship with Him?

_____

Now think about your own walk of faith. Mark your position on the scale to characterize your fellowship with God.

❋- - - - - - - - - - - - - - - - - - ❋ - ❋

Out of
fellowship

Vibrant and
growing

Having close fellowship with God doesn't guarantee that we will never sin again. However, when we disrupt our fellowship with God by sinning, we can repent and cry out for God to "create a clean heart" and "renew a steadfast spirit" in us (Ps. 51:10). When we do so, "He is faithful and righteous to forgive us our sins and to cleanse us from all unrighteousness" (1 John 1:9). Then our fellowship with Him is restored, and we are once again in a position to walk by faith.

When we disrupt our fellowship with God by sinning, we can repent and cry out to God.

How God Develops Consistent Fellowship

So far we've seen that God trains us to walk in fellowship with Him and that He guides us only through current fellowship with Him. Now let's explore the process God uses to develop the kind of fellowship He wants. The following diagram illustrates that process.

How God Develops Fellowship

Self-Orientation

God-Orientation

1. God teaches you His character, His purposes, and His ways.

3. Over time and through repetition God develops fellowship for a consistent walk of faith.

2. You must change your life to align it with God's revelation.

First, God begins teaching us what He is like (His character), what He wants to do (His purposes), and how He works (His ways). Second, we must respond by changing our lives in response to what we have learned about Him. These changes may include repenting of sin, incorporating Christian disciplines into your life, developing new friendships, ministering to others, spending more time with God, and so on. Third, when we respond to God over time and through repetition, turning to Him by faith becomes a habit. Let's look at the three steps by which God develops fellowship with Him.

God Teaches You His Character, His Purposes, and His Ways

To walk by faith, we must learn all three of these things about God. He will continually teach us these lessons until we operate from the platform of consistent fellowship with Him.

Learning God's character. One way we learn to walk in fellowship with God is to trust His character. God sought to work this truth into Jonah's life. One day God called Jonah to go preach to the Assyrians in their capital city, Nineveh. The Assyrians had become the world superpower of their day by conquering and subjugating other nations. Their cruelty knew little restraint. They ran fishhooks through the jaws of their captives and deported them to other lands. They pillaged and raped. They killed indiscriminately. They ripped open pregnant women. In short, they terrorized all of the lands around them. When Jonah received God's call, he immediately boarded a ship to set sail in the opposite direction of Nineveh.

7. Why do you think Jonah fled from this assignment?

_____

Interestingly, Jonah did not run because he was afraid. In fact, nowhere in the Book of Jonah did he ever demonstrate fear. He fled for a very different reason, which is finally revealed at the book's climax in chapter 4.

When the Ninevites repented after Jonah preached, God turned from destroying them. Jonah's anger boiled at God, and he said, "See? I knew You might do something like this! I didn't want them forgiven; I wanted them destroyed! That's why I ran in the first place! I knew You were a merciful and compassionate God, one who relents from destroying those who repent" (Jonah 4:2-3, authors' paraphrase). Jonah ran, not because he *lacked* faith in what God could do but because he *had* faith in what God could do. He unequivocally believed God could turn a phenomenally wicked people back to Himself in an instant, but he didn't trust God's character. He really didn't believe that whatever course of action God took would be best. God spent the rest of chapter 4 using a plant, a worm, and a scorching east wind to teach Jonah the lesson he very

God will continually teach us these lessons until we operate from the platform of consistent fellowship with Him.

much needed: true faith trusts that God's decisions are always best, even if they disagree with personal desires.

> **8. Have you ever been disappointed in God? Does He really know what He is doing? Are His ways really best? Would you embrace His character even if you don't understand His ways?** ○ Yes ○ No
> **If you have not been disappointed with God, stop and pray for someone who has.**

Many times God will not do what we want Him to do. We may earnestly pray that a loved one will not die, but he does; we may not receive the job we wanted; someone gets away with injustice; or we may earnestly plead with God to remove a thorn in our flesh, but He gently says no. At times like these a greater faith will yield to God's decisions, even if they contradict our desires. That's what it means to trust God's character.

In 1793 William Carey left the safety of England to go as a missionary to India. Over the next several months the friend who led him there abandoned him, Carey's five-year-old son died, his wife went insane and constantly attacked him, financial support from home dried up, and he couldn't find work because he didn't know the language. Not until seven years had passed did Carey finally see the first convert. By the end of his ministry, however, thousands had been converted, and millions of Indians have used his translations of Scripture. The principles Carey set forth for being a missionary blazed a trail for others, so that he has become known as the father of modern missions. Had his faith been only in God's power but not in His character, Carey would have given up long ago.

There will be times in your life when only faith in God's character will sustain you. You will set out to follow God, and things will not go as you expected. A cost may be required, or doubt will arise in your heart. At moments like these we must cast the anchor of faith into the waters of confusion. As Charles Spurgeon said, "When you can't trace His hand, trust His heart."[1]

> **9. Would you argue with God if He gave you a difficult assignment, or have you come to the place where you trust Him?**
> ○ Argue ○ Trust **Stop and respond to God in prayer.**

There will be times in your life when only faith in God's character will sustain you.

Learning God's purposes. Walking in maintained fellowship also requires learning God's purposes. Let's look at two interesting scenes from the life of the prophet Elijah. In the first scene he announced to King Ahab that God would send a drought on the whole land of Israel. Elijah certainly deserves high marks for his faith, but notice the audacity of his words: "As the LORD God of Israel lives, I stand before Him, and there will be no dew or rain during these years except by my command!" (1 Kings 17:1). What? How could he possibly believe that he could command the sky to rain or not? How could Elijah do that?

In the second scene Elijah stood on top of Mount Carmel in a showdown with all of the prophets of the god Baal—1 against 850 (see 18:19). He had proposed that they pray to Baal, and he would pray to Yahweh. The god who answered by dropping fire from heaven on the sacrifice would reveal who the true God was. If it were your prayer life, would you have confidence that God would create flames out of thin air when you asked? Could you honestly say, "I think I'll call a press conference because later today God is going to burn up this bull over here when I ask Him to"? How could Elijah do this? We glean the answer from part of his prayer in verse 37: "Answer me, LORD! Answer me so that this people will know that You, Yahweh, are God and that You have turned their hearts back."

Elijah had that kind of faith because He knew what God's specific purpose was. He understood that God desired to turn the heart of His people back to Himself. Knowing that his actions were in line with God's will, he could declare ahead of time what the fire would mean when it fell. Elijah was not showing off his prophetic powers. He was declaring what God was saying to the nation.

10. Would God reveal His purposes to you as He did to Elijah?
○ Yes   ○ No

> God will always reveal His purposes to those who are His because our ability to walk with Him depends on this.

Yes. God will always reveal His purposes to those who are His because our ability to walk with Him depends on this. The disciples usually missed Jesus' purposes. Almost everything they requested, Jesus did not do. He didn't send away the five thousand, Peter did not get to build three tabernacles, Jesus didn't christen James and John his number one and two men, He didn't allow the disciples to send the children away, and fire didn't fall on the Samaritans.

In contrast, in the Book of Acts the apostles received everything they asked for. What was the difference? They finally understood Jesus' purposes. Until they understood what the Lord's purposes were, they could not make the right requests. For this reason Jesus almost never answered them with a yes or a no. Instead, He answered in a way that would help them better understand Him and His purposes. When asked if they should call down fire from heaven on the Samaritans, He answered, "You don't know what kind of spirit you belong to. [You don't understand My purpose. This is My purpose:] For the Son of Man did not come to destroy people's lives but to save them" (Luke 9:55-56, note). Or when they asked to sit on His right and left, He asked if they could drink the cup that He would (see Matt. 20:22). Or when Peter tried to get Jesus to return to a village to address a crowd, Jesus told him He must go to other villages because "this is why I have come" (Mark 1:38). When they finally understood and trusted Jesus' purposes, it radically altered their actions and requests.

11. How long did it take Jesus to teach His disciples?
   ○ 3 days   ○ 3 months   ○ 3 years   ○ 30 years

Most scholars believe that Jesus' ministry lasted about 3½ years. It took time for Him to teach His disciples. Likewise, learning how to trust and incorporate God's purposes into our lives today takes time. Our fellowship with God grows as we increasingly alter our prayers and actions to align with His purposes.

Learning God's ways. A third way we grow in fellowship with God is to learn His ways. The Israelites who left Egypt perished in the wilderness because they refused to believe that God could give them the promised land. In Hebrews 3:10 God revealed at least one reason for their lack of faith:

> *They always go astray in their hearts,*
> *and they have not known My ways.*

Because the Hebrews didn't understand how God operates, their circumstances made them afraid. If they had learned that God leads us into the impossible so that He can demonstrate His power through us, the gigantic size of the land's inhabitants would not have intimi-

Our fellowship with God grows as we increasingly alter our prayers and actions to align with His purposes.

> *"To remain in the flesh is more necessary for you. Since I am persuaded of this, I know that I will remain and continue with all of you for your advancement and joy in the faith."*
> Philippians 1:24-25

dated them. If they had only understood that following God involves abandoning a comfort zone at some point, they might not have been so confused. Failure to grasp God's ways produced fear instead of faith. Conversely, the Apostle Paul could declare from prison that he would be released because he knew the Philippian church needed him (see Phil. 1:24-25). He knew God's using him was one of the ways God would build His church. Because Paul's release was vital to accomplish that, he prophesied his inevitable release.

12. Suppose God had given you biblical insights on missions, your heart was stirred when you recently met several persons who been on mission trips to Kenya, you unexpectedly received five hundred dollars, and you learned that your church was planning a mission trip to Kenya for two thousand dollars per volunteer. What would you expect to happen next?

○ I don't know. Should I expect something?

○ I would want to go, but I couldn't commit until I had the finances.

○ I would sign up and start looking to see how God would provide for me financially.

○ I would pray about whether to go.

Hopefully, you would sign up and start looking for God's provision of the finances. If God has been leading, you can be confident that He intends to complete something even if you don't yet know how. You can step out in faith because you know His ways.

13. Match each term in the left column with the correct definition on the right.

___ 1. God's character	a. The processes and methods by which God works
___ 2. God's purposes	b. God's attributes and personality traits
___ 3. God's ways	c. God's sovereign intent, desires, and goals

By trusting God's character (1. b), purposes (2. c), and ways (3. a), you allow God to grow your fellowship with Him.

You Must Change Your Life to Align It with God's Revelation

When God begins teaching us His character, His purposes, and His ways, we must make changes to align our lives with what He has taught us about Himself. We discover how thoroughly our lives center on our own selfish interests, preferences, and ways. When we enter a faith relationship with God, He begins to systematically tear down all of the things we have built in order to rebuild our lives on His truth. This process never ceases throughout our lives, but the changes are especially radical in the stage when God is developing consistent fellowship with Him. Just as a pendulum must swing downward before it can swing back up, our lives must travel downward before they can go upward. The required changes particularly take the forms of repentance and a reoriented lifestyle.

Change requires repentance. Repentance means *turning from sin.* Sin is anything that does not conform to God's character, purposes, or ways. God teaches us that His character is holy. When we find unholiness in ours, we must turn from it. In Psalm 2:8 God tells us that His purpose is to give the nations to His Son. When we realize that our primary purpose is to make enough money to retire early, we must repent and align our purpose with His. Perhaps He reveals to you that He accomplishes His will in a way that does not destroy relationships. If you realize that you seek to get your way regardless of what it does to others, you must repent. Every time you turn from sin, you travel down the pendulum arc. When you replace old patterns with godly ones, you travel up the pendulum arc. By repeating this process, you establish habits for maintaining fellowship with God.

Change requires a reoriented lifestyle. God will require changes in our lifestyle in order to walk in consistent fellowship with Him. This is certainly true for sinful areas of our lives but is equally true for areas that are not sinful. We may have to sacrifice some things— even good things—in order to go with God. If you work 60 hours a week but find that God wants you to spend intensive time in His Word getting to know Him, you may have to reduce the number of hours you work. If you enjoy Saturdays off but realize that the only way God can use you to impact your community is to coach soccer, you will have to change your priorities. You may find that God wants you to sleep one hour less so that you can pray, that He wants you

"Ask of Me, and I will make the nations Your inheritance and the ends of the earth Your possession."
Psalm 2:8

to increase your giving above your tithe, or that He wants you to call shut-ins in your church every week. Any of these examples would require you to rearrange your lifestyle in order to do His will and continue in obedient fellowship with Him.

> **14. Identify any areas of repentance or lifestyle changes that you feel God is asking you to make in order to develop your fellowship with Him.**
>
> _____
>
> **Write any commitment you are willing to make. If you are not ready, pray about areas of change God is showing you.**
>
> _____

Over Time and Through Repetition God Develops Fellowship for a Consistent Walk of Faith

A lesson learned does not become a lifestyle until it is repeated multiple times. In the same way, adjusting to God one time does not make a habit. He will cause us to practice lessons until they become second nature to us. Have you ever wondered why the God who controls the weather patterns allowed a life-threatening storm on the Sea of Galilee (see Matt. 8:23-27)? Circumstances don't just accidentally happen when we walk with Jesus. This was one lesson in a series. In Matthew 8–9 a centurion demonstrated great faith, Jesus asked where the disciples' faith was in the storm, a paralytic walked again through faith, a woman with an issue of blood was healed through her faith, and blind men received their sight through faith. God intentionally arranged these circumstances so that His Son could keep driving home the lesson of walking by faith until it became part of the disciples' lifestyle.

Adjusting to God one time does not make a habit. He will cause us to practice lessons until they become second nature to us.

> **15. Review the two lessons you listed in activity 2 on page 55. How many times did it take for you to learn them? _____**
>
> **What lessons are you still having to repeat? _____**
>
> _____

In summary, the process of developing consistent fellowship with God follows these three steps:

1. God teaches you His character, His purposes, and His ways.
2. You must change your life to align it with God's revelation.
3. Over time and through repetition God develops fellowship for a consistent walk of faith.

Throughout your life God will use this process to develop your fellowship with Him so that you can walk by faith. You don't experience the process for a few months and then become a sinless giant of faith. However, the orientation and inclination of your life will change from pleasing self to pleasing God. Don't be discouraged by shortcomings and failures. As long as you seek a consistent walk of faith, God will work in you to deepen your fellowship with Him, to grow your faith, and to accomplish His will through you.

> The orientation and inclination of your life will change from pleasing self to pleasing God.

Practicing Fellowship with God

We have examined the process by which God equips us to walk in fellowship with Him. Now we will describe six qualities that are forged by this process. These traits then help us continue to maintain current fellowship with God.

God-centered vision. Have you ever worn a pair of polarized glasses? The lenses are specially made to reduce glare by refracting the sun's rays. Interestingly, the refracted rays create the ability to see things indiscernible to the naked eye. Fishers often wear polarized glasses on a lake because the glasses allow them to see clearly under the water. To the naked eye, nothing but shimmering light dances off the surface, but an angler with altered vision can clearly see the fish below. In the same way, God must spiritually refract our natural sight to give us the ability to see as He sees.

No better example of spiritually polarized vision occurs than in 2 Kings 6. Elisha the prophet had enraged the king of Aram, Ben-hadad, by prophesying his battle plans to the king of Israel. Discovering that Elisha was in Dothan, Ben-hadad sent a massive army at night and surrounded him. In the morning when Elisha's servant witnessed the horses and chariots surrounding the city, he cried out in fear, "Oh, my master, what are we to do?" (v. 15). The natural vision with which he viewed the situation left no doubt that the lake water before him reflected certain doom. But Elisha answered, "Don't be afraid, for those who are with us outnumber those who are with them" (v. 16). They might have been looking at the same water, but he saw something very different than his servant did. The lenses he looked through revealed a reason for boldness. Then Elisha urged the servant to put on the glasses he wore so that the servant might see what he saw. Elisha prayed, "LORD, please open his eyes and let him see" (v. 17). So the Lord opened the servant's eyes; "he looked and saw that the mountain was covered with horses and chariots of fire all around Elisha" (v. 17).

16. What difference would it make if you could see as God sees the following circumstances?

A loved one unexpectedly dies: _____

_____

Ten new families move into your neighborhood: _____

_____

Your child faces adversity in school: _____

_____

A new job would require moving to another state: _____

_____

Having on the right set of glasses makes all the difference in the world. Both Elisha and his servant looked at the same thing but saw two radically different realities. If we do not wear God-centered glasses, we can never see what God wishes us to see. He will speak, but His voice will sound like an echo. He will do something in our circumstances, but we will be unable to discern what it means. He will paint a picture, but it will be too blurry to make out the image.

If we do not wear God-centered glasses, we can never see what God wishes us to see.

This is why the disciples could not comprehend Jesus' impending crucifixion, although He had repeatedly told them that He would die. Instead, Peter rebuked Jesus (see Matt. 16:22), James and John asked to sit at His right and left (see Matt. 20:21), and the twelve argued over who would be the greatest just hours before Gethsemane (see Luke 22:24).

Matthew recorded nine different occasions when Jesus foretold His death. If this were a one-time event, maybe we could understand why the disciples didn't get it. But nine times? Why were their eyes so blind? Because they viewed Him with the wrong kind of glasses. They saw the Messiah only through the natural lenses of their own self-made expectations. They thought He would be a conqueror, overthrow the Romans, and reestablish national sovereignty. In their lake water they saw only a reflection of worldly power, not a cross hidden beneath the waves. Our natural sight interprets everything according to our desires, experiences, purposes, and preferences. God-centered vision interprets our world from God's perspective, purposes, desires, and activity. This orientation to God puts us in a position to walk with Him by faith.

17. What can you do this week to move your view of life toward God-centeredness?
- ○ Listen to others to see where God is working
- ○ Ask God to give you His vision for viewing your circumstances
- ○ Draw closer to God through prayer and Bible study
- ○ Exercise faith to do something you know is God's will

Willingness. When God works in your life to develop your fellowship with Him, He seeks to work a willing spirit into your life no matter what assignment He gives you. Sometimes the excitement of the task causes us to chomp at the bit; sometimes the required sacrifice halts us in our tracks. When our heart hesitates, God has two choices: He can force us into submission through the superiority of His might, or He can persuade us to embrace a cross by showing us the benefits, rewards, and outcome that await us and others if we do His will. God prefers the latter. He begins to move in our hearts in such a way that we come to a place of willingness to obey Him in faith, so much so that we have joy in the midst of it.

"Peter took Him aside and began to rebuke Him, 'Oh no, Lord! This will never happen to You!'"
Matthew 16:22

"'Promise,' she said to Him, 'that these two sons of mine may sit, one on Your right and the other on Your left, in Your kingdom.'"
Matthew 20:21

"A dispute also arose among them about who should be considered the greatest."
Luke 22:24

"Rejoice in the Lord. To write to you again about this is no trouble for me and is a protection for you."
Philippians 3:1

"Rejoice in the Lord always. I will say it again: Rejoice."
Philippians 4:4

"Don't worry about anything, but in everything, through prayer and petition with thanksgiving, let your requests be made known to God. And the peace of God, which surpasses every thought, will guard your hearts and your minds in Christ Jesus."
Philippians 4:6-7

Paul spoke of his suffering and joy to the Ephesians as he ran the final lap of his life: "See, now I go bound in the spirit to Jerusalem, not knowing the things that will happen to me there, except that the Holy Spirit testifies in every city, saying that chains and tribulations await me. But none of these things move me; nor do I count my life dear to myself, so that I may finish my race with joy, and the ministry which I received from the Lord Jesus, to testify to the gospel of the grace of God" (Acts 20:22-24, NKJV). Peter and John shared the same spirit as Paul. When they were beaten for preaching the gospel, they rejoiced "that they were counted worthy to suffer shame for His name" (Acts 5:41, NKJV). Hebrews 12:2 refers to our Lord as "the source and perfecter of our faith, who for the joy that lay before Him endured a cross and despised the shame, and has sat down at the right hand of God's throne." God teaches us to have a mind-set that sees beyond the immediate. Because we know what He has done for us and what He will do through us, our faith enables us to sacrifice with joy.

18. Has God given you an assignment that requires sacrifice?
○ Yes ○ No

Joy and gratitude. Endurance and long-term service grow from gratitude and joy. Did you notice in Hebrews 12:2 that Jesus' willingness to go to the cross sprang from joy? The same is true for those who walk by faith today. Our heart does not naturally endure hardship with joy. We must deliberately exercise the heart like a muscle. Paul urged the Philippian church to work out the heart muscle.

19. Read the verses in the margin. Why did Paul tell the Philippian believers to rejoice and give thanks?
○ It's the spiritual thing to do.
○ It was easy for him to say because he had never suffered.
○ Rejoicing and giving thanks in all circumstances protect and guard our hearts.
○ If you are living the Christian life, it will always be easy to rejoice and give thanks.

Rejoicing and giving thanks guard our hearts when trouble or pain arises. Rejoicing and thanksgiving are not always emotional experiences, but the conscious decision to practice them reminds us of who God is and what He has done, is doing, and will do. Knowing the delights of who He is, the rewards that await us, and the good that God will do gives us faith to maintain a willing heart so that no one will rob us of our joy (see John 16:22).

> **20. Do you daily rejoice in who God is and thank Him for what He has done? Try thanking God for two to five minutes a day for a week to see the difference it makes in your life.**

Responsiveness. God rarely, if ever, reveals all of His work at once. Most of the time His will lies submerged like an iceberg, with only the tip showing. A key quality to discovering the 90 percent submerged beneath the surface is remaining responsive to what God has revealed to us so that we are always ready to obey Him in faith. After Jesus read in Scripture that His ministry was to be based around the Sea of Galilee (see Matt. 4:13-15), would He have discovered most of His twelve disciples if He had stayed in Nazareth? Would Peter have understood that God was going to save Gentiles if he had not gone with Cornelius's delegation (see Acts 10:1–11:18)? When Paul had a vision of a man in Macedonia asking for help, would he have seen conversions and a church being planted if he had stayed in Troas (see Acts 16:1-8)? Much of what God intends for our lives depends on our taking action by faith in response to what He has revealed.

The time to respond to the revelation of God's will is the moment He reveals it. Delay can cause us to miss all God has planned, and it usually carries tremendous consequences. When Jesus called the disciples, what would they have missed if they had decided on their own timetables? Would blind Bartimaeus have received his sight if he had not responded when Jesus passed by? When God told Joseph to flee to Egypt with Mary and Baby Jesus, how important was it for him to respond immediately? When God revealed to Paul's nephew that the Jews were plotting to kill Paul, could he afford to wait until the next week to respond? When God speaks, He wants us to respond immediately by faith.

Trusting God regardless of appearances. Many times in our faith walk, appearances can confuse us for two reasons:

"You also have sorrow now. But I will see you again. Your hearts will rejoice, and no one will rob you of your joy."
John 16:22

1. Events may occur, and we have no clue why they happen. These often prove painful and difficult if not impossible to understand.
2. We may hear a word from God; then everything looks as if it won't happen. We expect something to take place; yet nothing materializes, or a setback occurs.

Job, more than anyone else in the Bible, experienced terribly painful events for no apparent reason. Initially, God had blessed every area of his life due to Job's great righteousness; however, in one day he lost his entire wealth, his social standing, and all 10 of his children. These catastrophes were followed by an unimaginably painful illness that lasted several months. Such an immediate, deliberate reversal of fortunes gave the appearance that God was punishing him; yet Job could not think of anything he had done wrong. This situation greatly confused Job. Emotions of anger and trust, betrayal and faith illogically mingled together, erupting with each provocation by his friends, who accused him of secret sin. One side of his heart spouted accusations, mistrust, and suspicion. The other side clung to God in faith, hope, and integrity. Job 13:15, in the margin, expresses Job's inner turmoil.

> *"Though He slay me, yet will I trust Him. Even so, I will defend my own ways before Him."*
> Job 13:15, NKJV

21. If you are walking in fellowship with God, confusing circumstances happen, and God remains silent, what should you do?
○ Let the cross remind you that God loves you.
○ Remember biblical accounts showing that God always had a plan and brought good from it.
○ Let perseverance have its perfect work so that you can be mature, complete, lacking nothing (see Jas. 1:4).
○ All of the above

> *"Let patience have its perfect work, that you may be perfect and complete, lacking nothing."*
> James 1:4, NKJV

You would want to do all of these things to respond to God in faith even in the midst of difficult or misleading circumstances. Ultimately, God answered Job, restored double all of the possessions he had lost, and granted him 10 more children. His example of perseverance and his statement "Though He slay me, yet will I trust Him" (Job 13:15, NKJV) no doubt set an example for Jesus in enduring His crucifixion, as well as for millions of people through the years.

Other times we may think we know God's guidance; then something seems to block it. For example, perhaps you sense that God wants you to start a Bible study in your workplace. A number of people are excited, and you plan to begin in one month. Two unbelievers plan to attend. Suddenly, however, your company announces that you will be transferred to another state.

22. How would you interpret these circumstances?
- ○ God indicated His will, but you need to watch to learn where and how He will bring the workplace Bible study to pass.
- ○ You must have misunderstood God's will.
- ○ The company thwarted God's will.

In confusing circumstances like these, God is still at work. You probably didn't misunderstand God if He put the pieces together. A company certainly cannot thwart God's plans. Instead, you must watch and pray to see how He will bring this to pass. Maybe your first steps will inspire another believer to begin the study. Perhaps God will change the company's plans for you to move, or He might have prepared you to lead a workplace study where you are going. Because you maintain fellowship with God, you can watch with confidence to see how He will work this out.

Perseverance. Faith will always be tested. Passing the test requires perseverance and endurance. The greatest chapter on faith, Hebrews 11, is bookended by verses on endurance. The writer exhorted in 10:35-36, "Don't throw away your confidence, which has a great reward. For you need endurance, so that after you have done God's will, you may receive what was promised." He picked up again in 12:1, "Therefore ... let us ... run with endurance the race that lies before us." In the middle of chapter 11 we find this statement about Moses: "By faith he left Egypt behind, not being afraid of the king's anger, for he persevered, as one who sees Him who is invisible" (v. 27). This thread that runs throughout the book ought to grab our attention dramatically. At some point in your walk with God, you will have difficulties and temptations that urge you to give up, compromise, or take matters into your own hands. Waiting on God, clinging to Him, and believing what He has told you are necessary aids to walking with Him by faith.

You will have difficulties and temptations that urge you to give up, compromise, or take matters into your own hands.

23. Read the verses in your Bible and match each reference with the correct instruction on how to persevere.

___ 1. Romans 5:3; James 1:2-3   a. Look ahead to
___ 2. Romans 15:4   your reward.
___ 3. Colossians 1:11   b. Rejoice in affliction.
___ 4. Hebrews 10:35; 11:26   c. Be strengthened
                                        with God's power.
                                    d. Read the Scriptures.

These are great ways to grow in perseverance. The answers are 1. b, 2. d, 3. c, 4. a. Growing in perseverance equips us to walk by faith.

24. Review the six qualities that result from maintained fellowship with God. Shade each bar to represent the presence of that trait in your life.

	Slight degree	Moderate degree	Great degree
God-centered vision			
Willingness			
Joy and gratitude			
Responsiveness			
Trusting God regardless of appearances			
Perseverance			

When God initiates a faith relationship with you, He then spends a season in your life teaching you to maintain fellowship with Him. He retrains you to think and act by faith in Him rather than according to your preferences and desires. His work to reorient your life from self to God produces six important qualities that greatly help you walk by faith. The process usually takes time, but you can have joy and gratitude as you consistently walk by faith.

25. Fill in the blank in the margin to identify the second stage in a walk of faith.

A Walk of Faith

1. God initiates a faith relationship.

2. God develops _____ for a consistent walk of faith.

3. God requires a faith response to the unveiling of His will.

4. God matures faith through waiting.

5. God rewards completed faith.

1. Charles Spurgeon, as quoted by Rick Warren, "Quotes and Notes," *Rick Warren's Ministry ToolBox* [online], 4 April 2001 [cited 25 April 2006]. Available from the Internet: *www.pastors.com/RWMT/?ID=3.*

CHAPTER 4

God Requires a Faith Response to the Unveiling of His Will

After God initiates and develops a consistent walk of faith, a significant change occurs in the way He relates to you. In the first two stages God worked *in* you. Now He will begin working *through* you. God first laid a foundation for the way you are to relate to Him by faith; now He wants to impact your world through you.

This chapter will describe a very clear, four-step process for the way God usually works through you to impact the world as you respond to Him in faith. Because it is a process, God gradually reveals or unveils His will; it is progressive in nature. You do not see His will all at once but step by step along the way as you walk by faith. As He unveils His will, you must respond correctly in faith. When you do, God's power will work through your life to impact others in ways only God can do.

How God Works with Us

Before we trace the process by which God reveals His will to us, we need a foundational understanding of the way God works with believers. We can identify four basic truths about the interplay between the revelation of God's will and our faith response.

God first unveils His will to you. Ordinarily in Scripture God first told someone He was going to do something before He did it. For example, God revealed to Noah that He would judge the world. God involved Abraham step by step from Ur to Mount Moriah. God progressively revealed Himself to Isaac, Jacob, Joseph, Moses, Joshua, judges, kings, and prophets. In each instance God clearly told them what His will was.

In the New Testament Jesus is the preeminent example of a faith walk. He said, "The Father who lives in Me does His works" (John 14:10). At Pentecost the Holy Spirit took up residence in each believer with the specific assignment to guide us, teach us, bring to our remembrance all He has told us, and reveal God's will to us (see John 14:26; 16:13; 1 Cor. 2:10). Throughout Acts the Spirit unveiled God's will to Peter, John, Stephen, Paul, Barnabas, and others.

The scriptural pattern is for God to unveil His will to people before carrying it out. With confidence we know that He still works the same way today. Before God does a mighty work where you are, He will tell you or someone near you what He has planned.

> **1. Reread the previous sentence. Do you believe that God will work that way in your life?**   ○ Yes   ○ No

God will work with you the same way He worked with believers in Scripture to reveal and carry out His will.

God then unveils His will through you to bless others. God has a purpose for revealing His will to you. When He told Moses that He wanted to deliver His people, He did so because He wanted to accomplish it through Moses. When God called Paul on the Damascus road, His primary desire was to work His will through Paul. God's purpose in revealing His will to these men was to impact others for His kingdom. The focus of the burning bush was not the bush but

---

"The Counselor, the Holy Spirit— the Father will send Him in My name—will teach you all things and remind you of everything I have told you."
John 14:26

"When the Spirit of truth comes, He will guide you into all the truth. For He will not speak on His own, but He will speak whatever He hears. He will also declare to you what is to come."
John 16:13

"God has revealed them to us by the Spirit, for the Spirit searches everything, even the deep things of God."
1 Corinthians 2:10

deliverance for the Israelites. The focus of the Damascus road was not the blinding light but the Gentiles who would be saved. When God speaks, do not focus on the experience of God's revealing His will to you; focus on His purpose—on what He will do through you.

After God tells you His will, He begins to unveil through you the steps by which He will accomplish it. God told Moses at the burning bush that He would deliver His people and bring them into the promised land. Then God unveiled through Moses the steps He would use in the process: inflicting 10 plagues, parting the Red Sea, making a covenant at Sinai, and leading the Hebrews to the Jordan River. God told Paul on the Damascus road that he would be a light to the Gentiles and stand before kings. Then God unveiled Paul's missionary journeys and his appearance before King Agrippa and Caesar as the means of bringing about His purposes. As Moses and Paul walked with God, He progressively unveiled His will through them in order to bless others.

> After God tells you His will, He begins to unveil through you the steps by which He will accomplish it.

2. Check the two statements that are most accurate.
- ○ 1. The unveiling of God's will refers to a step-by-step process in which God works through you to accomplish the result He desires.
- ○ 2. The unveiling of God's will refers to the result He wants.
- ○ 3. When God reveals His will, it comes from Him to you.
- ○ 4. When God reveals His will, it comes from Him to you in order to impact others.

The answers are 1 and 4. God works through you to bring about His will, and His purpose is for you to impact others for His kingdom.

God unveils His will through you when you remain in the flow of a consistent walk of faith. In order to experience God's will through our lives, we must be in position to respond correctly. Baseball coaches teach Little Leaguers that the first step in making a play is to put their bodies in position to catch and throw the ball. If the players are not squared up with a grounder or if they aren't under a fly ball, they will make an error. In the same way, we must be in position for God to unveil His will through us.

The two diagrams on page 80 show Christians who are in position and out of position to hear from God and respond to Him by faith. The box in the diagram on the left represents the guidelines God has set for fellowship with Him. Inside those boundaries God's blessings continuously flow—the revelation of Himself, the unveiling of His will, His answers to prayer, His peace, His power, His joy—everything that is available to us from God by faith. The diagram on the right illustrates a burned-out Christian who is outside the boundaries of maintained fellowship. To experience God unveiling His will in and through us, we must get in the flow.

In the Flow of Maintained Fellowship with God

Within the boundaries of maintained fellowship, blessings flow from God through you to bless others.

Outside the Flow of Maintained Fellowship

3. Check the best answer. Being in the flow means—
- ○ 1. having mystical, mountaintop experiences with God;
- ○ 2. walking in consistent fellowship with God as He unveils His will through us;
- ○ 3. being faithful in church attendance and Christian duties;
- ○ 4. being orthodox in all major Christian doctrines.

The correct answer is 2. The diagram on the left represents a Christian who consistently walks in fellowship with God. As we stay in step with Him, He unveils His will through our lives. He speaks to us, guides us, and works through us. The joy of experiencing a dynamic relationship with God is what Jesus meant by *abundant life* in John 10:10: "I have come that they may have life and have it in abundance." When we are connected and walk in step with the Father, we experience this life in ever-increasing measure as we function by the guidelines He has set for fellowship with Him.

However, we can easily step outside the flow of God's activity when we live outside the guidelines God has established for fellowship with Him. This situation is represented by the diagram on the right on page 80. We may drift, get distracted, revert to doing things the way we have always done them, become lazy, or trip over other stumbling blocks. When this happens, we no longer experience the abundant life God intends for us. Notice the circular pattern in the diagram. In this state we spin our wheels from one activity to another. We feel burned out, exhausted, and unfulfilled. We know something is amiss but may not be quite sure what. Church life leaves us chasing our tails, hoping we can discover God's will but feeling empty. Until we get in the flow, we cannot know God's will or the joy God intends for our lives because we cannot experience God's presence outside the guidelines He has set for consistent fellowship with Him.

Worse yet, when we are outside the flow, we cannot influence others for Christ. The world does not see His power demonstrated in our lives. Operating in our own abilities and strengths, we cannot do God's will, because outside the flow *we do not know His will.* Therefore, it is imperative for the sake of God's kingdom that we know how to discern the Father's will and then align our actions with it.

The unveiling of God's will through you requires a faith response. In Scripture God rarely did anything for people without requiring a response on their part. For example, Joshua had to march around the city of Jericho 13 times before the walls fell (see Josh. 6:1-5). God did not heal Naaman until he had washed himself 7 times in the Jordan River (see 2 Kings 5:14). God did not rebuild the walls of Jerusalem until Nehemiah came, organized the people, dealt with enemies, and corrected oppression among his own people. Why? Couldn't God have torn down the walls of Jericho without having the people march around it? Couldn't He have healed Naaman when he washed the first time? Couldn't He have ordered an angel to repair Jerusalem? Of course He could. But He rarely works that way. God does not do everything for you. Instead, He requires that you respond to Him. To experience God unveiling His will through you, you must be proactive in responding to His work in your life.

> We can easily step outside the flow of God's activity when we live outside the guidelines God has established for fellowship with Him.

God requires not only a response but also a response of faith. In the Bible God neither led by sight nor told people all details about what would happen ahead of time. He always led people beyond their own capacity or logic, and He normally told them only one step at a time. Their willingness to follow in faith determined whether they experienced God. What do you suppose would have happened to Naaman if he had balked at washing in the Jordan River? What if Joshua had thought marching around the city was a stupid military strategy? What if Nehemiah had decided that going to Jerusalem was too much trouble? Would they have experienced the fulfillment of God's will through their lives? God would have accomplished His will anyway, but the honor would have gone to others. They would have forfeited the joy of being instruments through which God's will came to pass. They would have missed God's best for their lives.

> God always led people beyond their own capacity or logic, and He normally told them only one step at a time.

4. Check the statements that are true.
- ○ 1. God delights in including us in His work.
- ○ 2. We must respond in order to experience God unveiling His will.
- ○ 3. Our response to God requires faith.
- ○ 4. Our self-confidence grows when God works through us.

All of these are true except 4. When we respond in faith and see God work through us, our confidence in Him, not confidence in ourselves, grows. He accomplishes His will through us because it brings Him pleasure to include us in His work. God requires that we respond in faith to experience the unveiling of His will through our lives.

How God Unveils His Will

The accomplishment of God's will through your life requires God's initiative and your cooperation. Typically, this interplay of God's work and your faith response occurs in a four-step process:
1. Your faith is *activated* by a word from God. You can't dream up something yourself, call it a word from God, and expect Him to bless it.
2. Your faith is *enacted* by believing God. Faith without works is dead (see Jas. 2:26).

3. Your faith is *visualized* by watching for God. You see God putting together all of the pieces necessary for His will to come about.
4. Your faith is *finalized* by acting on the opportunity God sets before you. After God has put all of the pieces in place, He carries out His will through you when you respond.

5. Number the following four steps in their proper order to see an example of how God unveiled His will in and through the disciples' lives to impact others.

_____ They spent more than three years with Jesus being discipled, became convinced He was the Messiah, learned guidelines for living in His kingdom, experienced the work of the cross and resurrection, and were endued with power when the Holy Spirit came on them at Pentecost.

_____ Immediately they left their nets and followed Him.

_____ They preached, and three thousand were saved at Pentecost.

_____ Jesus said, "Follow Me, and I will make you become fishers of men" (Mark 1:17, NKJV).

Jesus' word to "follow Me" *activated* the disciples' faith. Their faith was *enacted* when they believed Him and left their nets. They *visualized* God putting all of the pieces in place—discipleship; conviction that He was the Messiah; the work of the cross and resurrection; and finally, receiving the Holy Spirit. When the Spirit came, the last piece was in place, and the disciples' faith was *finalized* as they acted on the opportunity God had set before them. As a result, God accomplished His will of salvation for three thousand souls through the disciples at Pentecost. Answers: 3, 2, 4, 1.

Now we will look at each step in detail. We will illustrate the four steps by showing how they unfolded in Jesus' life and by building on the diagram we introduced earlier (see p. 58).

Your Faith Is Activated by a Word from God

Jesus never initiated anything. Period. He did not try to do God's will without receiving a word from His Father. Rather than invent things to believe God for, Jesus waited until the direction from God was clear (see John 5:30; 12:49). Neither can believers today base our faith on what we decide we want to do for God. In the following

> "I can do nothing on My own. I judge only as I hear, and My judgment is righteous, because I do not seek My own will, but the will of Him who sent Me."
> John 5:30

> "I have not spoken on My own, but the Father Himself who sent Me has given Me a command as to what I should say and what I should speak."
> John 12:49

diagram step 1 is the starting point where God's will begins to flow or begins to be unveiled through you.

1. Your faith is activated by a word from God.

This pattern holds true for other people of faith. The phrases "The word of the Lord came to ...," "according to the word of the Lord," and "the Lord said" occur numerous times in Scripture, indicating that God's direct communication triggered someone's faith. Two truths need to be explained about receiving a word from God.

God activates our faith by a specific word from Him. In each biblical example in which God revealed His will to someone, the person had a specific word from God, not just a general word from Him. A significant difference exists between a general word from God and a specific word from God. A general word sets the basic guidelines and boundaries of God's will. A specific word, on the other hand, tells you how to act in a specific situation. For example, God gave Joshua a general word to conquer the promised land. The general word set the direction for Joshua; however, he had no clue how that general word applied to taking Jericho (see Josh. 6:1-5). Then God communicated to Joshua a specific word to march around the city. Joshua and the people acted on that word (vv. 6-20), and God completed what He initially said (vv. 20-21). God's specific word activated Joshua's faith for a specific instance to fulfill His general word.

Hebrews 11 gives other examples of faith that was activated by a specific word from God. We are told that Noah did not move until he was "divinely warned of things not yet seen" (v. 7, NKJV). Abraham obeyed "when he was called" (v. 8, NKJV). Regarding the promise of a son, Romans 4:20-21 records that Abraham "did not waver at God's promise through unbelief, but was strengthened in faith, giving glory to God, and being fully convinced that what He had promised He was also able to perform" (NKJV). Sarah was strengthened because of what God had promised (see Heb. 11:11). Each had a specific word from God that set his or her faith in motion. Thus, they were able to speak of unseen things as being present realities.

This pattern reflects the way God's Spirit uses the Bible. Scripture is a general word that sets the standard for the way Christians relate to God, one another, and the world. The Spirit takes the general word of God and applies it specifically in your life. For example, the general word of God says, "Be fruitful and multiply" (Gen. 8:17), but nowhere does the Bible tell you whom and when to marry. You need a specific word from God for that. Jesus knew from Scripture that He would choose twelve disciples, but nowhere in the Old Testament did it give Him their names. He knew from Scripture that He would perform miracles, but Scripture never spelled out walking on water or feeding the five thousand. He knew that He was the resurrection and the life, but He didn't know when to teach that to His disciples until Lazarus died. The general word from God needed to be applied by a specific word from God.

As you maintain consistent fellowship with God, you will learn to recognize the Spirit's voice when He gives specific guidance.

> *"By faith even Sarah herself, when she was barren, received power to conceive offspring, even though she was past the age, since she considered that the One who had promised was faithful."*
> Hebrews 11:11

6. Draw lines across the columns to match the general word from God with the related specific word from God.

- Train children in the way they should go.
- Make disciples of all nations.
- Serve one another.

- I am going on a mission trip to Asia this year.
- Our men's group repaired homes of single mothers in our church.
- The solution to the negative influence of my son's peer group was to involve him in wholesome activities.

Unfortunately, some Christians make at least two errors in regard to a word from God:

1. Some protest the assertion that we must have a specific word, saying things like "God wants to save all the lost; that's specific enough." However, as we have seen, this is not the pattern of

Scripture. Twice the Spirit of God forbade Paul from evangelizing in certain places in order to go to Macedonia (see Acts 16:6-10).

2. Some people act without a word from God. The Word of Faith (name it and claim it) movement does not err in emphasizing the requirement of faith but in omitting God's role in activating that faith. In Word of Faith theology, people are the chief initiators, actors, and determiners of their actions. We supposedly have the power to decide, name, and claim what to believe God for instead of receiving a specific word from Him. Much of Word of Faith speech revolves around the use of personal pronouns in phrases like "I speak my faith into being," "I say to this mountain," "I claim"—*I, I, I.* Word of Faith adherents further assume a formulaic, cause-and-effect to walking by faith. They claim that if they do A, B, and C, then they are guaranteed a certain result for whatever they desire. They view faith as a scientific equation rather than a relationship with a Person.

Other people get a feeling and act on it without taking time to make sure it was from God. When He doesn't bring it to pass, they conclude that it wasn't God's will. When they say God is leading them but then change their story, they imply that their failure is God's fault for not completely showing them what steps to take. Most likely, they never had a clear direction from God to begin with, or they mishandled their word from God.

7. Mark the following statements *T* (true) or *F* (false).

_____ 1. Word of Faith (name it and claim it) theology leads people astray by emphasizing the necessity of faith for God to work.

_____ 2. It's not a big problem to say you know God's will and then backtrack when God doesn't bring it to pass.

_____ 3. Word of Faith (name it and claim it) theology leads people astray by interpreting certain verses on faith to mean they can get whatever they decide they want.

The answers are 1. *F,* 2. *F,* 3. *T.* Believers are not to initiate their course of action. Always wait for God to activate your faith by giving you a specific word for what He wants you to do.

Hearing God's specific guidance can make all the difference in walking by faith. I (Lonnie) experienced this truth when God called me to another church. The effectiveness of the visitation program I inherited was marred by church members who spoke disparagingly of members who didn't participate. What should have been a blessing had become a hindrance to our unity. I had a dilemma. I knew God's general word from Scripture was to evangelize. Although at my previous church God had gloriously saved many people through the visitation program, I sensed God leading me to cancel this one and instead teach people how to evangelize their friends and co-workers in their everyday lives. That course of action required faith; however, God blessed and saved more people in our church that year than in any other year in my tenure. God's specific guidance led us to practice evangelism in a specific way.

8. Name a time when God gave you a specific word that activated your faith.

_____

God's specific word is often subtle and usually relates to people. We are not usually called on to build arks, move to a faraway land, or birth children past childbearing years. Instead, God often communicates with us in seemingly small ways. Suppose you are a homemaker. God puts it on your heart to call your neighbor and ask whether she has a need. You find that she desperately needs to run an errand and cannot take the children. When you keep the children for her, God uses you to meet the need but also gives you an avenue for communicating His love to a neighbor. What just happened? You just got in the flow of God's activity.

Perhaps you are a factory worker and a co-worker is having a difficult financial problem. God directs you to help the co-worker. When you obey God, the co-worker asks why you wanted to help. God just opened a way for you to proclaim Jesus. You just got in the flow. Small? No, in God's kingdom it is monumental when He gives you a specific word.

Jesse Tharpe, a pastor in Tennessee, heard about a ministry to the poor. One day God spoke to him to pray for the needs of that ministry. When He obeyed that still, small voice, he called and discovered that they needed a tractor-trailer truck to go to Georgia to pick up shingles for roof repair. Next he shared the prayer

In God's kingdom it is monumental when He gives you a specific word.

request with the people in his church. One woman in the congregation was married to a truck driver. She called him and told him of the need. He replied that he would go get the shingles and transport them to the ministry. God used Jesse, a woman, and her husband to procure a truck and deliver the roofing. Through this small obedience to God's leading, hundreds of people have been helped, scores of houses have new roofs, and many people have come to faith in Christ. God's subtle leading to Jesse was to pray. God's completed will was for multitudes to be impacted and many saved.

9. Which two statements best reflect the previous truths?
   ○ A word from God is always audible and dramatic.
   ○ God's word often relates to people.
   ○ God's speaking is often subtle.
   ○ When God speaks subtly, it's because the thing
      on His heart is minor.

God's work often relates to people and is subtle. He may speak to you through your daily Bible reading. Perhaps a specific word will come to you through circumstances, a preacher, a Sunday School teacher, a friend, or a child. At times He may prompt your heart by the Holy Spirit. God can speak in a million different ways, but your life must be ready so that you will detect His prompting. Many Christians pray that God will do something good for them, but they don't listen for His answer. To hear that answer, we must align our hearts with His. Once we are on the same frequency, we will know how to respond in faith when He shares His heart with us. Often God helps us get on His agenda by placing a hunger in our hearts. When He does, we ought to rejoice! God never causes a hunger that doesn't carry with it His abiding promise:

> *Blessed are those who hunger*
> *and thirst for righteousness,*
> *because they will be filled.* MATTHEW 5:6

A hunger from God is His announcement to you that He intends to speak to you to reveal His will.

A hunger from God is His announcement to you that He intends to speak to you to reveal His will.

10. Identify a hunger God has given you in order to activate your faith and reveal His will.

_____

God activates your faith by a word from Him. That word is specific and usually relates to people. God sometimes speaks dramatically, but more likely, His word to you will be subtle. God's word to you leads to a second step in the process by which He reveals His will.

Your Faith Is Enacted by Believing God

When Jesus received a word from His Father, He always believed what the Father said, and He always responded. No wonder one description of Jesus' character in the Gospels is "powerful in action" (Luke 24:19). He went to Capernaum, healed, taught, performed miracles, called disciples, traveled, oversaw a ministry to the poor, swiftly handled conflict, and did a host of other things because of what His Father had said to Him about His ministry. If Jesus had done nothing in response, He could have been accused of having no faith at all. However, once Jesus heard His Father in prayer, He didn't stay in the prayer closet. He went into the world, where the Father began to work through Him to impact others. His faith was enacted when He believed His Father and responded.

> When Jesus received a word from His Father, He always believed what the Father said, and He always responded.

GOD

1. Your faith is activated by a word from God.
2. Your faith is enacted by believing God.

> "What good is it, my brothers, if someone says he has faith, but does not have works? Can his faith save him? If a brother or sister is without clothes and lacks daily food, and one of you says to them, 'Go in peace, keep warm, and eat well,' but you don't give them what the body needs, what good is it? In the same way faith, if it doesn't have works, is dead by itself. But someone will say, 'You have faith, and I have works.' Show me your faith without works, and I will show you faith from my works. For just as the body without the spirit is dead, so also faith without works is dead."
>
> James 2:14-18,26

11. Read the passage in the margin. Check any applications you could draw from this passage.
- ○ 1. Faith allows me to separate my personal convictions on Sunday from the way I live the other six days of my life.
- ○ 2. Faith allows me to say I believe that God can take care of me financially but not tithe.
- ○ 3. Faith allows me to believe that God is the One I ought to follow but refuse to move to another location.
- ○ 4. If I truly believe, the evidence will be a response that is consistent with my belief.

The answer is 4. You will respond to what you believe to be true. Let's explore what it means to enact our faith by responding to God.

The essence of belief is acting in commitment to what we perceive to be true about God. If we really believe God, we will act in commitment to Him. Faith cannot believe a fact without acting on that fact: "Faith is the reality of what is hoped for, the proof of what is not seen" (Heb. 11:1). Although Abraham didn't know where he was going, he left his home when God told him He would make him into a great nation and bless the whole earth through him (see Gen. 12:1-4; Heb. 11:8-10). His actions revealed his faith. In Luke 17, 10 lepers came to Jesus and begged Him for mercy. He gave them a specific word: "Go and show yourselves to the priests" (v. 14). They believed Jesus and acted on His word. Then this amazing statement follows: "While they were going, they were healed" (v. 14). Can you see the pattern? They received a word from God, they believed His truth, their belief resulted in action, and God's will came to pass. In the same way, you must take action when God speaks to you in order to see Him work through you.

Conversely, when our faith fails to act in commitment to God's Word, we do not see the demonstration of God's power. In Matthew 13 Jesus returned to His own country, but people began to question His authority. Verse 58 records, "He did not do many miracles there because of their unbelief." Their lack of faith canceled the possibility of seeing the Savior change their lives. Hebrews 3:8-19 also confirms this truth with a warning: "Watch out, brothers, so that there won't be in any of you an evil, unbelieving heart that departs from the living God" (v. 12). The writer referenced the Israelites, who failed to believe God in the wilderness, and commented on the consequences of their unbelief: God was provoked with them for 40 years, their bodies fell in the wilderness, and they could not enter His rest. He cautioned his readers, "We see that they were unable to enter because of unbelief" (v. 19). The Hebrews' failure to act in commitment to God's word canceled all God intended for their lives. He then waited to accomplish His will through their children.

12. Indicate whether you agree or disagree with this proverb: "After you pray, you must put feet to your prayers."
○ Agree   ○ Disagree   **Explain your answer.**

_____

This proverb usually holds true as long as we are careful to wait until God has spoken before we act. By responding in faith, we show that we believe what God has shown us to be true.

When God speaks, we must immediately respond in faith. Not only must we act on what we believe to be true, but we must also act immediately. God has a timing factor in His will. We cannot act when we feel like getting around to it. Failure to capitalize on the window of opportunity may short-circuit what God intends to do through our lives. The moment God speaks is the moment to respond.

An immediate response first begins in the heart. Believing must precede acting. For example, when God told Abraham that He would make him a great nation, Abraham could do nothing at that moment. Instead, he believed God, and it was credited to him as righteousness (see Gen. 15:6). There would be actions to take later to do God's will, but initially things were set in motion merely by Abraham's immediate heart response. Consider your own salvation. Did your actions of commitment occur before you believed or after? They were after. You believed, then confessed Christ publicly, were baptized, and began seeking to live a lifestyle pleasing to Him.

If possible, your immediate faith response should additionally be expressed in an overt action. Although this sometimes isn't possible, it usually is. When Paul received word on the Damascus road that he would stand before kings one day, he couldn't do so at that moment. However, he took overt action by immediately withdraw-

> By responding in faith, we show that we believe what God has shown us to be true.

ing to the Arabian desert to prepare himself. Those three years laid a foundation on which God kept building until one day He placed Paul before Caesar. When God speaks to you, stop and identify what action you should immediately take to respond in faith.

13. What has God recently spoken to you about? _____

_____

Do you believe the word God has given you enough to act in faith? ○ Yes ○ No

What immediate response do you need to take? _____

_____

To enact your faith, you must believe that what God said is true, that He will do what He said, and that you will be blessed by seeing it come to pass. When action follows belief, your faith is set in motion.

When action follows belief, your faith is set in motion.

Your Faith Is Visualized by Watching for God

The third step in the process of God's revealing His will in response to faith can be illustrated in Jesus' death on the cross. In step 1 God gave His Son a specific word that He would accomplish redemption through Him. In step 2 Jesus believed Him and immediately began responding. Notice what happened in step 3. Jesus' faith worked

GOD

1. **Your faith is activated by a word from God.**
2. **Your faith is enacted by believing God.**
3. **Your faith is visualized by watching for God.**

with and waited on God for His will to come about. Jesus seemed to have an internal trigger that guided Him when to act and when not to act. For example, at times He delayed or refused certain actions encouraged by his mother and brothers, saying, "My hour has not yet come" (John 2:4) and "My time has not yet arrived" (7:6). Here He crouched in the starting blocks with a word from God, muscles taut to spring into action, but until the right moment He held back, awaiting the crack of some mysterious starting gun known only to Him. Then suddenly, His Father must have fired it. Something signaled to Jesus that God's timing had arrived. He exploded off the blocks and began crying out, "The hour has come" (12:23; 17:1). How did Jesus know what to do when?

> **14. What is the best explanation of how Jesus knew when to do God's will?**
> ○ 1. He's God. He knows everything.
> ○ 2. He probably prayed about it, then felt led.
> ○ 3. He knew when He saw God put in place the last piece of the puzzle showing it was necessary for Him to die.

The answer is 3. Jesus knew what to do because He visualized the activity of the Father. By *visualized* we do not mean a New Age technique but seeing God work before our eyes. Let's explore what it means to visualize faith.

Watch for God to put in place the pieces that are necessary for His will to come about. Jesus knew when His hour had or had not come because He observed whether His Father had put all of the pieces in place that were necessary for His will to be accomplished. As Jesus watched, His Father dropped at least three things in place signaling that the cross was imminent:

1. Jesus never spoke of the cross until Peter declared, "You are the Messiah, the Son of the living God!" (Matt. 16:16). Once the Father had worked in the disciples' hearts to convince them of this fact (see Matt. 16:17), Jesus knew His time was short. He spent the rest of His ministry with them speaking about the cross.
2. Jesus saw the disciples' discipleship process drawing to a close. On His last night He declared it complete: "I have glorified You on the earth by completing the work You gave Me to do. I have

Jesus' faith worked with and waited on God for His will to come about.

revealed Your name to the men You gave Me from the world. The words that You gave Me, I have given them" (John 17:4,6,8).

3. When these pieces were in place and the Passover approached, Jesus knew it was time to die as Scripture had foretold.

When we receive a word from God, we must start watching constantly to see what God begins to do around us.

15. Based on Jesus' example, which statement more accurately describes God's usual pattern?
- ○ He gives us a word and then mysteriously makes it happen in its final form.
- ○ He gives us a word and then puts the pieces in place over time.

We sometimes think that God will give us a word and then mysteriously make it happen in its final form. Usually, this is not the pattern He uses. We, like Jesus, must watch and respond as we walk in faith while God puts the pieces in place. Three years ago God spoke to me (Lonnie) and some others about creating a teen center to minister to the youth in Lynch, Kentucky, where we live. We had no money, no resources, and nobody to run it. We had no clue how, when, or where this ministry would be carried out. Nevertheless, we had a word from God, so we began watching to see how He would put the pieces together. One day a church from Spartanburg, South Carolina, called and asked, "Is there a dream or vision we could help you with?" I shared my heart about the teen center. "What do you need?" they inquired. I listed a number of items, such as game tables, seats, and audio equipment. "That's no problem," they replied. "We would love to do that." There it was! Piece number 1 of the puzzle.

Instantly we began to discuss what the Lord might want for the teen center and to watch for God's further activity. The church began collecting the necessary items to put in the center, but we still had no place to meet and nobody to run it. Later I met two young men who wanted to volunteer their time that summer. I shared with them the need to influence teenagers. They had worked with youth before and enthusiastically asked to serve. There it was! Piece number 2.

Two weeks before the Spartanburg team was to deliver supplies, we still had no facility for the teen center. Then suddenly a pharma-

When we receive a word from God, we must start watching constantly to see what God begins to do around us.

cist and his wife, Charles and Julie Boggs, sold their pharmacy and moved to another location. Dr. Boggs came to me and said he had an extended lease on the now-vacant building that he must honor. "Could you use it in ministry?" he asked. "I will give it to you." There it was! Piece number 3. Now we had a building, personnel, and equipment for the center. Our faith was visualized as we watched God put the pieces together. Each time He did, we acted. Now Club 180 is a reality, ministering to the teens in our area.

16. Check ways you can watch for God to put the pieces in place, based on Lonnie's story.
   ○ 1. After you believe God, you must figure out what to do next.
   ○ 2. You must actively watch for God.
   ○ 3. One way to watch is to listen for and ask what God has put on others' hearts.
   ○ 4. You must proceed in faith at each critical juncture and continue watching for the Father's activity.

All except 1 are examples of ways faith is visualized. Jesus, the master of watching where the Father was expressing His activity, lived in constant awareness of what the Father was up to. One day Jesus was walking down a street in Jericho and saw a man sitting in a tree. He immediately stopped and said, "Zacchaeus, hurry and come down, because today I must stay at your house" (Luke 19:5). What was happening? Why would Jesus stop a procession to speak to a complete stranger? Jesus realized that only God could prompt a rich, successful man to climb a tree just to see Him. He acted to find out what His Father was doing by going to Zacchaeus's home. The conversation resulted in Zacchaeus's repenting of a sinful lifestyle, restoring fourfold what he had stolen, and giving away half his goods to the poor (see v. 8). Jesus then declared, "Today salvation has come to this house" (v. 9).

Jesus' vigilance caused Him to visualize the Father's activity unfolding before His eyes. Likewise, if our faith is to visualize God putting the pieces of His will together around us, we must watch for Him in the ordinary events of our daily routines. He is working in every circumstance, meeting, and relationship, bringing you to see His activity around you. As you drop off the kids at school, be aware

> We must watch for God in the ordinary events of our daily routines.

95

of His presence. As you work in the office, be aware of His will. As you play golf with friends, be aware of His activity. As you close a business deal, be aware of His resources.

17. Where can we most often find God revealing His will?
○ Special, sensational events   ○ Daily routine

Check your answer in the previous paragraph.

Interpret your circumstances in light of what God is doing in your life. Your faith is visualized not only when you watch for God but also when you begin to interpret your circumstances from a different point of view. If you are in the flow of God's activity, every circumstance you encounter will not be a hindrance to doing God's will but will bring you closer to the completion of His will. How did Jesus interpret the "setbacks" of His arrest, suffering, and crucifixion? Scripture frequently says these things were done so that the words of prophecy "might be fulfilled" (John 15:25; 18:32; 19:28). In spite of the appearance of things, God's will was being accomplished. For those who walk by faith, every circumstance further enlightens them to know how to pray and act.

Paul interpreted his circumstances in this fashion: "I want you to know, brothers, that what has happened to me has actually resulted in the advancement of the gospel, so that it has become known throughout the whole imperial guard, and to everyone else, that my imprisonment is for Christ" (Phil. 1:12-13). Amazing! The things that happened to Paul were to complete God's will where Paul was at that time.

How do you interpret your circumstances after you hear a word from God? Do you immediately say, "This cannot be God's will" instead of seeing occurrences in light of God's work in your life? Do you determine God's will by what you thought would occur, or do you open your mind to understand how God is at work in what is actually happening? Do you, like Peter, begin to doubt, so that God can do no mighty work where you are because of your unbelief? Faith believes when circumstances do not match expectations. Faith acts as though what God said is reality, not will be reality (see Heb. 11:1).

"Faith is the reality of what is hoped for, the proof of what is not seen."
Hebrews 11:1

18. Number these phrases in their proper order to summarize the way God works in your circumstances.

____ Every circumstance will not be a hindrance to God's will

____ If you are in the flow of God's activity

____ To bring you closer to the completion of God's will

____ But further enlightens you in how to pray and act

The correct order is 2, 1, 4, 3. It may take a while to train your mind and heart to watch constantly for God's presence and to interpret circumstances correctly. You may find yourself once again acting before God has put all of the pieces in place or doubting because of the way things appear. However, through practice and perseverance God will teach you how to overcome old thoughts and habits as He grows your faith and uses you mightily.

> Through practice and perseverance God will teach you how to overcome old thoughts and habits as He grows your faith and uses you mightily.

19. What circumstances in your life indicate that God is putting the pieces together to fulfill a word He gave you?

_____

_____

If you don't see God's activity, what will you do?

○ Forget about it. God has decided not to follow through.

○ Walk by faith and watch for God to act.

○ Give up, assuming you were wrong about receiving a word.

Your Faith Is Finalized by Acting on the Opportunity God Sets Before You

Once the pieces are in place, we must take appropriate action for God's will to be finalized through our lives. When Jesus saw the last requirement fulfilled for Him to die, He immediately put Himself in position for the crucifixion. By His action God accomplished salvation through Him. In the case of the teen center, our faith was finalized when we launched the ministry. Once God set all of the pieces in place and we acted on the opportunity set before us, our faith became a reality, and God used our ministry to build His kingdom and to bring glory to Himself.

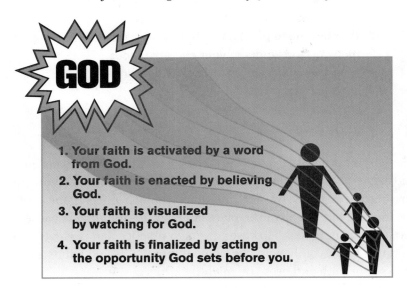

20. True or false? "Your faith becomes finalized" is another way of saying that God's will is completed through you.
Circle your answer: True   False

When your faith is finalized, God completes His will through your life.

The answer is true. When your faith is finalized, God completes His will through your life.

The four-step process we have examined by which God reveals His will can be seen in Philip's life.

21. Read Acts 8:26-40 in your Bible. Identify the events in Philip's life that correspond to the four faith steps we have studied.

Faith activated: _____

Faith enacted: _____

Faith visualized: _____

Faith finalized: _____

In step 1 God *activated* Philip's faith by saying, "Get up and go south to the road that goes down from Jerusalem to desert Gaza" (Acts 8:26). In step 2 Philip's faith was *enacted* when he responded in faith by going, although he did not know what God would do. In step 3 the reason for God's command became clear when Philip *visualized* God at work in an Ethiopian eunuch. In step 4 Philip's faith was *finalized* when he acted on the opportunity set before him. God's will was completed through Philip when he finalized his faith by witnessing to the man and God saved him.

> **22. Identify a time when God completed His will through you in the following ways.**
>
> Faith activated: _____
>
> Faith enacted: _____
>
> Faith visualized: _____
>
> Faith finalized: _____

Walking by Faith

When God sets an opportunity before you, He may require you to do things you've never done. For example, God led me (Lonnie) to begin a food ministry, a teen center, and a housing ministry for several thousand people a year, although I had never done any of these things before. Sometimes our hearts can be intimidated by the challenge God sets before us. Remembering three truths about faith greatly strengthens our hearts and our resolve to walk by faith.

1. *Wherever faith leads you, God will already be there.* When Belinda and I moved to Lynch in 1999, we shared with our new church what God had spoken to our hearts. A woman stood up, tears streaming down her face, and said she had been walking the streets for 11 years praying that God would send someone to help. God was already there a long time before we arrived!

2. *Faith will never ask you to do what God hasn't already equipped you to do.* All your life God molds you, sets patterns for His work through you, and prepares you for His glory to be revealed through you. One time a man came to our area, observed our ministries, and concluded that he could start a ministry where he lived. He

Faith will never ask you to do what God hasn't already equipped you to do.

had always loved cars his entire life and had raced on a dirt track years before. He returned home and started a dirt-track church that on last report had three hundred in attendance.

3. *Faith will never ask you to give what God Himself will not provide.* In Philip's case God provided water in the desert for baptism at the precise moment it was needed (see Acts 8:36). God charged the disciples to feed the five thousand, then provided the answer Himself through five loaves and two fish (see Matt. 14:17). In Lynch we sensed God's call to feed hungry people in the mountains. We could not do that, but we could pray and trust God to provide. He answered by sending us food from many different sources. Today we annually distribute approximately three hundred thousand dollars in free food yet have never once requested a single penny. When God asked us to help people with shelter, clothing, and other needs, He sent thousands of volunteers and the necessary resources to accomplish His will. Our God is an awesome God!

A Walk of Faith

1. God_____
   a faith relationship.

2. God develops
   _____
   for a consistent
   walk of faith.

3. God requires a
   _____
   _____
   to the unveiling
   of His will.

4. God matures faith
   through waiting.

5. God rewards
   completed faith.

23. What are three truths that encourage us to accept the challenge God sets before us?

1. Wherever faith leads you, _____
   _____ .

2. Faith will never ask you to do what _____
   _____ .

3. Faith will never ask you to give what God Himself _____
   _____ .

Remember that when God gives you a word, He does it not for your sake but for others. His primary focus is not to bless you but to make you a blessing. Believers are sometimes tempted to focus more on God's activity *in* us than *through* us. However, the process of God's working in us is merely the means to the result the Father wants. If you love others and want to get in the flow of God's purposes, God will unveil His will in your life in order to impact others. Will you get in the flow of God's activity? Will you allow God to speak a word to you and accomplish it through you as you respond in faith?

24. Fill in the blanks in the margin to identify the first three stages in a walk of faith.

CHAPTER 5

God Matures Faith Through Waiting

Today sonograms allow people to peek into a world unknown to previous generations. For the first time in history, bioimaging has made it possible to see the gender and growth of a baby in the womb. Doctors can measure skull diameter, see spinal development, and pronounce the child a boy or a girl. However, they cannot do it all at the same time. They must change the location and depth of the sonogram wand to bring into focus the different parts of the baby they wish to view before getting the entire picture.

In the three previous chapters we have waved the wand of Scripture over different stages or elements of faith development to bring into focus different aspects of that process. We learned how God initiates a faith relationship with us by radically intersecting our lives. We examined how He develops fellowship for a consistent walk of faith. We observed how the unveiling of God's will and your faith response work together to bring about His purposes in and through your life. Now we bring into view a stage in your faith walk that is crucial to maturing faith. If we move our sonogram wand over the lives of biblical giants of faith, we see one more requirement for walking with God by faith.

Waiting Is Integral to Faith

As God develops our faith, He takes us through an unusual experience to mature us. Looking at the different images of the sonogram printout of faith, we begin to notice a peculiar pattern in the lives of Bible characters. As we examine the first image, we wonder how much time elapsed from the moment God told Noah He would flood the world until it happened. At a minimum it was the length of time required to build an ark—possibly 120 years. Now look at the second image and notice the time between God's promise to make Abraham a great nation and his son's birth—25 years. In the third image we see that 22 years passed from the time Joseph dreamed that he would rule over his family until it happened. The fourth image reveals 40 years Moses spent in the desert before God finally delivered the children of Israel through him. Moving down the printout, we learn the answers to these questions: How long was it from the time Hannah first prayed for a son until God granted her one? Several years. How long was it from the time Samuel anointed David king until he assumed the throne over all Israel? From his boyhood to age 37. How long was it between Paul's call and his first missionary journey? Probably 11 to 14 years.

1. What can we learn from this pattern?
   - ○ God worked more slowly back then.
   - ○ Nothing. The way God worked with people in the Bible doesn't mean He will work that way with us.
   - ○ There will also be times of waiting in our lives after receiving a word from God.
   - ○ That's the way God works with truly spiritual people.

All saints of the Bible experienced waiting as an integral part of the growing faith process.

All saints of the Bible experienced waiting as an integral part of the growing faith process. Sometimes the waiting lasted only a few days, as when the 120 tarried in the upper room until the promised Holy Spirit came or when Paul went to Macedonia and very quickly saw a church birthed. Sometimes the waiting lasted for years. But the point is this: after receiving a word from God, you will experience a period of waiting for God to fulfill His word. This may not happen every time, but it will no doubt happen multiple times in your life.

Let's look at four important facts about this period of waiting.

God has a purpose for waiting. Has God ever delayed an answer to your requests longer than you thought necessary? Maybe you asked, "Where are You, God? Don't You care? Why don't You answer me?" Have you ever wondered whether the biblical giants of faith faced these same howling inner voices of doubt while they waited on God? What must have Joseph thought in slavery and prison? What went through Moses' mind during 40 years in exile? How did David react to being pursued by Saul? Surely these men must have faced doubts, but evidently, God placed in their hands a sword of truth to slay these giants. David wrote in Psalm 138:8, "The LORD will fulfill His purpose for me." This statement reveals that David learned two things while waiting for God to act. First, God has a purpose for the waiting period. Second, by using the word *fulfill,* David assumed it was a process of waiting over time. David believed that God always has a purpose for waiting.

2. What purposes might God have for wanting us to wait?

_____

_____

You could have named a number of purposes. We thought of four purposes God has for the waiting period:
1. God is glorified.
2. A believer gains a deeper knowledge of God and greater faith in God.
3. A believer develops godly character.
4. God prepares other people to receive His will.

David's life illustrates these four purposes of waiting:

> After receiving a word from God, you will experience a period of waiting for God to fulfill His word.

1. As David patiently endured persecution by Saul and as God delivered him on several occasions, God was glorified. Even Saul glorified God by confessing that the kingdom would one day become David's (see 1 Sam. 24:20). David's life also mirrored Jesus' life in many ways, thus reflecting the glory of the coming Messiah.
2. David also experienced a much deeper knowledge of and faith in God during waiting by choosing to constantly rely on Him. For example, during this season of life he wrote numerous psalms about the Lord as Deliverer.
3. God developed His character in David through waiting. David's forgiveness of others and faithfulness especially reflected God's character. God regarded David as "a man after My heart, who will carry out all My will" (Acts 13:22).
4. God used David's period of waiting to prepare others to receive His will. As David waited more than 20 years to become king, more and more people understood that God's will was for David to be king. As a result, all Israel backed David's becoming king with no political fallout or bloodshed (see 1 Chron. 12:38).

God has the same purposes for allowing times of waiting in your life. Accept these periods as God's preparation to be glorified, to bring you to a deeper knowledge of and faith in Him, to conform you to His character, and to prepare those around you to receive His will through His work in your life.

Waiting on God is the most challenging stage of faith. When you stand in the middle of your need or circumstances, strong temptations will arise to take matters into your own hands. Many times people who mishandled God's will in the Bible did so because they succumbed to pressure to act without Him. In his old age Abraham sensed that God wasn't moving fast enough to provide a son, so he and Sarah came up with their own solution. Sarah adopted a practice common in that day for women who were sterile: she gave her maid, Hagar, to Abraham to become pregnant so that the child born through Hagar would be considered Sarah's son (see Gen. 16). They succeeded in obtaining a son, Ishmael, by their efforts, but the results were cataclysmic. Ishmael's descendants and the Jews have been in conflict for centuries, up to the present day.

"All these warriors, lined up in battle formation, came to Hebron with wholehearted determination to make David king over all Israel. All the rest of Israel was also of one mind to make David king."
1 Chronicles 12:38

King Saul faced an invading army. When the prophet Samuel didn't arrive to offer sacrifices to seek God's help, many of Saul's men began deserting in fear. As pressure mounted, Saul assumed the role of priest and offered the sacrifices. Because God's law prohibited such an action, Saul lost his kingdom (see 1 Sam. 13:3-14).

In contrast, Bible characters who overcame the challenges of waiting saw God's mighty power. To walk in faith, you must learn how to wait on God.

3. Describe a time when you had to wait on God to fulfill a word He had given you.

_____

_____

How did you react to this waiting period? _____

_____

Maybe you were surprised by the need to wait for God to act. This dimension of faith is perhaps one of the least acknowledged in modern Christianity. Our society has been conditioned to expect instant gratification, on-demand service, and frenetic activity. We have instant coffee, tea, hot chocolate, oatmeal, and rice. We pop dinners, soup to go, or popcorn into the microwave and sometimes don't even wait for the microwave to finish. Our society feeds on fast food, and even then we grow impatient in the drive-through lane. No longer is e-mail fast enough; now we require instant messaging.

We want things immediately to fulfill the endless list of duties and activities before us. We are a society ablaze in constant motion. Most of us rush from one event to another, consumed by a blitzkrieg of chores, responsibilities, and duties. This conditioning subtly spills over into our relationship with God. Most of the time we don't wait for a word from God, but if we hear Him, our default is to crank up the organizational machine to help Him out. We list all of the steps involved and put them on a timeline of our choosing, which is generally as fast as possible. However, God doesn't work on the basis of the instant but on the basis of eternity. He doesn't work on the basis

> Most of the time we don't wait for a word from God, but if hear Him, our default is to crank up the organizational machine to help Him out.

The priorities
of eternity and
meaning require
different concerns,
methodologies,
and strategies from
those to which we
are accustomed.

of activity but on the basis of meaning. The priorities of eternity and meaning require different concerns, methodologies, and strategies from those to which we are accustomed.

4. Which statements reflect a concern with eternity and meaning?

○ 1. I have only a short amount of time, so I must cram in as much as I can.

○ 2. What I do in this life will last in the next, so I can trust God to choose the direction, pace, and way that are best.

○ 3. Meaning in life consists in the activities I do and the things I acquire.

○ 4. Meaning consists in relationships with God and others; therefore, I will act on a timetable and in a way that yield abundant life in relationships.

Numbers 2 and 4 align with God's concerns for eternity and meaning. When we successfully respond to the challenges of waiting on God, He accomplishes what will have maximal impact for eternity and relationships.

Let me (Lonnie) share the way God used a challenging time of waiting to build my faith. When God began sending hundreds of mission volunteers to Lynch, we needed a suitable place they could stay. We began to pray that the Lord would provide a mission house for the volunteers. As I began watching for God to unveil His will, I noticed an empty, 12-room house across the street. We began praying that God would give it to us. At this point we had a choice. We could go to the bank and apply for a loan to purchase the home, or we could wait for God to provide the funds. Because we didn't believe that He was guiding us to go into debt at that time, we waited on Him in the confidence that He would provide the funds.

After 2½ years of praying in faith, the house was sold to someone else. We thought we had missed God's will, but shortly after that, God sent a mission team to our area. One of the volunteers, who specialized in property renovation and resale, noticed an old hospital standing vacant. He offered to buy this 4-story, 27,000-square-foot, 69-room building and lease it to us for one dollar a year! Suddenly God showed us that He wanted to give us a 69-room building instead of a 12-room house. I immediately tracked down the land company that owned it, gave the contact information to the investor, and waited in anticipation. Three months later I received a phone call. The deal with the company had fallen apart! A company representative had called to let me know they would soon sell the building.

5. How would you have reacted to this circumstance if you had been confident that you had a word from God?
- ○ State my intent to buy it and trust God to provide
- ○ Immediately get a loan to buy the building so that I wouldn't lose it and miss God's will
- ○ Be upset with God for dangling a carrot in front of me, only to snatch it away
- ○ Do nothing, concluding that it wasn't God's will after all or wasn't His timing

I told the man not to sell the building because I believed God wanted to use it in the mountains for His glory. He asked me, "Do you really believe that?" I confidently answered, "Yes." He replied, "Then why don't you buy it?" I asked what he wanted for it. He answered, "$85,000." That was an incredible bargain, but I didn't even have $850. However, I told him that my Father was rich and would buy the building for us. The man graciously said he would give us 30 days to get the money. We did not begin fund-raising but prayed and waited, for I knew if God was guiding, it wasn't my responsibility to make it happen by my own ingenuity.

Over the next three weeks we received $25,000 out of the blue from various sources. The company agent called one week before closing to ask me if I was ready. At that point I had to make a decision. By all appearances I was not ready, but the money God had already sent signaled His intent to provide. "Yes," I replied. That weekend my wife received a call from a man in Ohio saying he felt God impressing him to give to our ministry. He wired money to us that arrived the day of closing—a check for $65,000! God had provided, and the building was His! Through this experience we were blessed to realize the truth of 1 John 5:14-15: "This is the confidence we have before Him: whenever we ask anything according to His will, He hears us. And if we know that He hears whatever we ask, we know that we have what we have asked Him for." God led us this way to increase His glory and to mature our faith.

If God was guiding, it wasn't my responsibility to make it happen by my own ingenuity.

6. What resulted in Lonnie's life from responding in faith to the challenge of waiting? Check all that apply.
○ God was glorified because everyone knew He did it.
○ All involved in the process grew in faith and intimacy with God.
○ He received something better than he had originally prayed for.
○ His joy was greatly increased.

All of these blessings resulted from Lonnie's willingness to wait on God. God accomplished immeasurably more through his waiting than through instant gratification.

To wait on God, we must reject the tendency to walk by sight. Paul asked the church in Galatia three penetrating questions: "I only want to learn this from you: Did you receive the Spirit by the works of the law or by hearing with faith? Are you so foolish? After beginning with the Spirit, are you now going to be made complete by the flesh?" (Gal. 3:2-3). In effect Paul was saying, "Hey! Think about it! Have you lost your mind? If you started out by faith/the Spirit, what makes you think God wants to change horses in midstream?" Little wonder Paul told the Corinthian church how he and his team had chosen to live their lives: "We walk by faith, not by sight" (2 Cor. 5:7).

Why did Paul need to remind believers of something so fundamental to the Christian life? Because human beings' natural inclination is to walk by what we see, hear, and feel. This knee-jerk reaction stems from four sources.

1. Most powerfully, we all lived our lives this way before conversion. Scripture calls this pattern living "according to the flesh" (see Rom. 8:4-5,12-13; Gal. 4:23,29). After conversion this nature coexists with our new nature in Christ throughout our earthly lives. The greatest challenge a Christian faces is to be constantly filled with the Holy Spirit day by day so that we walk in the Spirit and not in the flesh.

2. We tend to imitate the models we deem successful. For example, around 1000 B.C. the children of Israel decided to adopt the system of government common to all of the nations around them. Although God warned them of the consequences, they persisted in asking for a king, to their detriment. Instead of walking by faith in God, the Hebrews wanted to install a visible power figure in whom they could place their trust (see 1 Sam. 8).

"... in order that the law's requirement would be accomplished in us who do not walk according to the flesh but according to the Spirit. For those whose lives are according to the flesh think about the things of the flesh, but those whose lives are according to the Spirit, about the things of the Spirit."
Romans 8:4-5

3. Formal education teaches us to make decisions based on empirical (observed) evidence without seeking God's perspective. Although formal education carries indispensable benefits, it also teaches us to rely on the world's standards, methods, and ways rather than God's if we do not filter out those messages.

4. Believers have adopted many of the world's standards, methodologies, and ways. Our tendency when we receive a word from God is to immediately put a strategy into place to make sure that word comes to pass. Someone may say, "God gave us a mind to use; let's use it." This statement is usually a call to do God's business using our own wisdom.

> **7. Considering our tendency to walk by sight rather than by faith, check the true statement about human planning.**
> ○ Planning should be done only in response to God's direction.
> ○ Planning should be minimized because it tends to undercut living by faith.

Planning is not to be minimized. Spiritual leaders in Scripture always planned but only in light of God's direction. The ark required great planning and organization, but God gave Noah the boundaries in which to do it. Delivering a nation, building a society, and providing for the people required a lot of preparation by Moses, but God set the guidelines for it. If you take cues from the flesh, feelings, or sight, you will try to do God's will the world's way. Either you will get a good idea and then plan your strategy to make it happen, or you will get a word from God but not wait on Him. Depending on your skill level, you may even see some success; however, God is under no obligation to support your efforts. In the long term you will find that the responsibility for maintaining the ministry or idea rests on you, and it can become frustrating, time-consuming, and difficult.

If you take cues from the flesh, feelings, or sight, you will try to do God's will the world's way.

> **8. Think about a time when you sensed that God wanted you to do something for Him. How did you respond?**
> ○ Rushed out and started, only to find later that I didn't have enough money, personnel, or materials to maintain what He said to do
> ○ Waited to act until God had put the pieces of His plan in place

When God gives a word and you wait for Him to put the plan together, the responsibility for the idea or ministry rests on Him. He always provides all you need to bring about His will. When God begins something, He also maintains it until its completion. Philippians 1:6 says, "I am sure of this, that He who started a good work in you will carry it on to completion until the day of Christ Jesus. Philippians 2:13 adds, "It is God who is working in you, enabling you both to will and to act for His good purpose." If God starts it, He maintains it; if you start it, you maintain it.

If God starts it, He maintains it; if you start it, you maintain it.

9. **What are areas of your church life in which it would be particularly important to have a word from God and go about it His way? Examples include launching a building campaign, changing worship-service style, and starting a new ministry.**

_____

_____

Learn to live with an unmet need or desire. Growing up, were you impatient waiting for Christmas and your birthday? Were you anxious to get your driver's license? Probably so, if you were like most of us. Were you just as anxious to get vaccinations? What about having your braces tightened or eating liver and onions for supper? If you were like most kids, you could have easily waited your entire life for those things. The difficulty in waiting rises in proportion to the strength of your need or desire. When God delays in fulfilling a need or desire, you will be tempted to take matters into your own hands. Therefore, to wait on God, you must learn how to live with an unmet need or an unfulfilled desire.

One of the greatest biblical examples of waiting can be seen in the life of David. He had a word from God that He would be the king of Israel because the current king, Saul, had disqualified himself through disobedience (see 1 Sam. 15:23; 16:12-13). Saul responded by seeking to take David's life, although David had done only good for him. David was driven into the desert, hunted, persecuted, dishonored, and forced to endure many other difficulties. Saul's actions generated numerous needs and desires in David's life, such as safety, vindication, deliverance, and food. On two occasions David had an opportunity to kill Saul, thus fulfilling those needs his way instead of God's, but he refused (see 1 Sam. 24; 26).

10. Why do you think David was able to resist the temptation to take matters into his own hands?

_____

One fundamental quality of David's faith enabled him to wait on the Lord—anticipation. Once you have a word from God, you know He will bring it to pass. You don't have to worry about it or try to make it happen. Instead, you can enjoy what will be although it has not yet come to pass. Suppose good friends from out of town called to let you know they would visit you soon. You have not yet experienced the pleasure of their company; you must wait for their arrival. However, you are filled with joy in anticipating that time. While enduring years of persecution, David placed his faith in God and anticipated the day God would place him on the throne. His expectancy of that fact strengthened him to wait on God to do His work His way.

> Once you have a word from God, you know He will bring it to pass. You don't have to worry about it or try to make it happen.

I (Lonnie) had to wait three years for the Lord to bring about the housing needed for our mission volunteers. In the early days we were forced to provide makeshift lodging in unusual places. This chaotic, changing, less-than-ideal situation created extra work and headaches for us; however, I was filled with joy in the meantime by anticipating what God would do. Along the way He taught us other valuable lessons about living with an unmet need.

1. Although we weren't comfortable with the situation, God was actually meeting our need. Too often we confuse need and convenience. We cry out to God to provide when we really want Him to make it easy. In this deception we sometimes live in the future so much that we miss God's provision in the present. God was providing for us, but it just required work.

2. As our need increased, His provision increased. When we had only six hundred volunteers, we didn't need the hospital. God waited to give us the building when the other provision could no longer support the growing number of volunteers.

3. The way we responded during this time determined whether we experienced God's provision and glory. Had we acted prema-

turely, we would have been stuck with a 12-room house and a lot of debt. The 12 rooms would have been inadequate to accommodate our needs, and we would still have struggled to provide housing. The pressure to jump was great, but when we waited on God, He provided something far better in a way that showed everyone watching that He did it!

11. Answer *T* for *true* or *F* for *false*.

_____ You can live with an unmet need even though you haven't disciplined your mind to trust God to provide.

_____ Successfully waiting with an unmet need requires believing the truth of God's promises.

_____ Many times God has provided, though it might not be at the comfort level we desire.

Have you ever taken matters into your own hands instead of waiting on God? Describe what happened.

_____

_____

Waiting in faith requires believing God's promises and trusting Him for provision, even though we may not be comfortable.

Waiting in faith requires believing God's promises and trusting Him for provision, even though we may not be comfortable. The answers are *F, T, T.*

Waiting on God Requires Active Seeking

We've established that God has a purpose for waiting and that it is the most challenging stage of your faith walk. You must reject the tendency to walk by sight, and you must learn how to live with an unmet need or desire. These realities raise an interesting set of questions: What does waiting on God look like? How do you wait on God, what do you do while you wait, and what can you expect to experience during waiting? When you go to the doctor's office, you usually have to wait. You sit around reading magazines or watching TV—doing nothing but wasting time and hoping you will be called next. Waiting on God isn't like that. Don Miller correctly stated, "There are no chairs in God's waiting room."[1] You are not idle but are very involved as the Father brings His word to pass. Jesus described your responsibility in waiting this way: "Keep asking, and it will be given to you. Keep searching, and you will find. Keep knocking, and the door will be opened to you" (Matt. 7:7). You must take action in the process of waiting on God.

Ask until you have clarity. Once you hear God's word to you, you must begin asking and keep asking until He clarifies what He specifically desires. When the mission-team volunteers began coming, I (Lonnie) recognized that God was saying that He wanted to use them to make an impact on our area. The word He spoke through His activity informed my praying. I immediately began asking Him to meet the need for housing. When the 12-room house came to my attention, I prayed for it for more than two years because at that time it seemed the best option. When it sold, I went back to God to ask for clarity. When the hospital came to my attention shortly afterward, God's Spirit suddenly confirmed in my spirit that this infinitely better provision was what He intended. When the property investor was unable to purchase the building but the land company wanted to sell, I knew to ask for the $85,000 directly from God.

12. Based on the example, how should you actively wait on God through asking?
- ○ 1. I find what looks good, ask God for it, and then sit back until He does it.
- ○ 2. I actively pay attention to God's activity and continually adjust my prayers, based on the way He leads, until I understand what He intends.
- ○ 3. If I get enough of my friends to agree with me (see Matt. 18:19), God will hear our prayers despite circumstances.

God usually works according to statement 2. The whole time in the waiting process, I actively paid attention to God's activity and continually adjusted my prayers until I understood how God intended to provide. In the end God met my needs in a better way than I had imagined and glorified Himself in the process.

"If two of you on earth agree about any matter that you pray for, it will be done for you by My Father in heaven."
Matthew 18:19

Seek specifically and expectantly. Each time after you ask, watch for God to direct the people or circumstances to you that fit your request. This type of seeking carries two assumptions.

1. You must know specifically what you are looking for. In Luke 15:4-9 Jesus told parables about a man searching for a lost sheep and a woman hunting for a lost coin. In both cases they knew exactly what was missing. Some people seek in such vague terms that if God answered them, they wouldn't know it. When you say, "I'm seeking God's will for my life," you need to ask yourself, *What am I seeking to know about His will? How would I know if God answered me with such a hazy prayer? Am I now searching for the opportunities He will place in front of me to serve? Or am I expecting God to miraculously and instantly do it?* If you do not know what you are looking for, you could have it and not know it!

2. You must keep looking until you find what you are seeking; otherwise, you really didn't expect to find it. The man and the woman in Luke 15 persevered because they anticipated recovering what was missing; otherwise, they would not have begun looking. You too must be expectant. You will not seek something if you believe there is no possibility of finding it.

> **13. Is faith required if we don't know what we are seeking or we don't seek it expectantly?** ○ Yes ○ No
> **Why or why not?**
>
> _____
>
> _____

Faith is not required if we are not specific or expectant. If we had not been seeking housing, faith would have never been applied to buying the old hospital. If we had not expected God to provide, we would not have declared to the land company that God would give us $85,000 in a month.

As you knock, keep doing what God has called you to do. Think for a moment about knocking on a door. First, do you knock when a door is open or closed? Knocking assumes a closed door; God has not yet provided. Second, if you keep knocking, as Scripture instructs, what

Faith is not required if we are not specific or expectant.

kind of time span does that assume? Matthew 7:7 implies that you will go back to the door again and again over a prolonged period.

What do you do until God opens the door? Asking for clarity and seeking specifically and expectantly are two components of the process, but there is also a third. You must be busy doing either the last thing God told you to do, whatever it takes to meet the needs at hand, or both. In the case of housing volunteers, we needed a place to put the mission teams who were coming. We asked God to open our eyes to how He would provide, then expectantly started seeking His answer. In the meantime we found temporary solutions in empty church basements, apartments, and houses. We cleaned them, put down mattresses, and built a bathhouse in the local park for volunteers to take showers. We did this every year for three years. All the while the number of volunteers increased until we reached two thousand in one summer! Were we idle while we were waiting? Not at all. We often worked 14- to 16-hour days meeting the needs of the mission teams.

"Keep asking, and it will be given to you. Keep searching, and you will find. Keep knocking, and the door will be opened to you."
Matthew 7:7

14. Number the following statements in the order that reflects active waiting.

____ In the meantime I must actively do whatever it takes until the long-term need is met.

____ I start asking and searching to see how God will provide.

____ God gives a word that identifies a need.

The order is 3, 2, 1. We knew that God was sending volunteers. We began asking and searching in faith for a long-term provision for housing, then did whatever was required in the meantime. As we waited on God, we continued to do what we were called to do. In the end God gave us a 69-room retreat center.

15. If you are waiting for God to act, are you asking until you have clarity?   ◯ Yes   ◯ No

Are you seeking specifically and expectantly?
◯ Yes   ◯ No

As you knock, are you continuing to do what God has called you to do?   ◯ Yes   ◯ No

You Will Be Tested While You Wait

In this chapter we have learned that walking by faith requires waiting and that waiting on God does not mean inactivity but hard work. We have still another vital truth to learn about the way faith grows through waiting.

I (John) studied the words *test, tests, tested,* and *testing* in the Bible and discovered something shocking: sometimes Satan tests us, but in the vast majority of cases it is God who tests us. In fact, God promises that He will test us. He declared in Jeremiah 17:10,

> *I, the LORD, examine the mind,*
> *I test the heart*
> *to give to each according to his way,*
> *according to what his actions deserve.*

God tested Abraham when He asked him to offer his son Isaac (see Gen. 22:1). He led the children of Israel into the wilderness for the express purpose of testing them (see Deut. 8:2). He withdrew from Hezekiah to test him, to know his heart (see 2 Chron. 32:31). In fact, every person in the Bible who received a word from God was tested in the waiting period that followed. Likewise, if you walk by faith, you will be tested.

16. Read Hebrews 12:1-13 in your Bible. What is the spiritual mind-set that God wants us to have toward His discipline?
○ Endurance   ○ Reluctance   ○ Resistance   ○ Fear

What is the fruit of God's discipline (see vv. 10-11)?

_____

The writer of Hebrews instructed us to run the race with endurance, looking to Jesus, "the source and perfecter of our faith, who for the joy that lay before Him endured a cross and despised the shame" (Heb. 12:2). James 1:2-4 tells how to respond when God tests us: "Consider it a great joy, my brothers, whenever you experience various trials, knowing that the testing of your faith produces endurance. But endurance must do its complete work, so that you may be

"Remember that the LORD your God led you on the entire journey these 40 years in the wilderness, so that He might humble you and test you to know what was in your heart, whether or not you would keep His commands."
Deuteronomy 8:2

mature and complete, lacking nothing." God's goal in testing us is to produce holiness, peace, and righteousness in our Christian walk.

An attitude of endurance, submission, and joy will help you respond like Joseph and not like Jacob when you are tested. God gave Joseph a word that he would rule over his family one day, and he excitedly told his brothers and father. It immediately generated conflict with his brothers and a mild rebuke from his father. His infuriated brothers eventually responded by selling him into slavery, then schemed to cover up their evil deed by telling their father that wild animals had devoured Joseph. Although Scripture records that Jacob had kept Joseph's dream in mind (see Gen. 37:11), he chose to believe the lie his sons told rather than the truth God had revealed through Joseph. Too often this can be our response when a test arises. The enemy can bring all sorts of experiences into our lives to deceive us from believing the word God spoke. Jacob spent years mourning the untruth that his son was dead but not a single day rejoicing that the Lord said Joseph would reign. Joseph, on the other hand, believed what God said was true and never wavered in slavery or in prison. He waited in the assurance that God is able. If Joseph had lost hope, he would have fainted in testing and would have missed God's purpose for his life.

17. Have you chosen to believe an untruth over God's truth?
   ○ Yes   ○ No   **If so, how do you need to respond?**

_____

_____

Let's examine common challenges we may face when tested during a time of waiting.

Confusing circumstances. When God unveils His will, it doesn't always come to fruition in logical ways. God's seemingly illogical process can cause confusion and second-guessing if you fail to interpret your circumstances in light of what the Lord has said. You must especially keep your eyes on God during this time. Remember Joseph's circumstances on his way to ruling Egypt? First he was thrown into a pit (see Gen. 37:24), then sold into slavery (see v. 28),

> God's goal in testing us is to produce holiness, peace, and righteousness in our Christian walk.

then condemned to prison (see Gen. 39:20). How would you have viewed these events? If you look only at circumstances, you can get confused about seeking and recognizing God's activity in your life.

The circumstances of the cross brought great confusion to the disciples' lives, but did that change God's will? No. Later they recalled Jesus' teachings about His death and resurrection and were liberated by them.

When we did not have a large enough building for volunteers, did this mean we were not to host volunteers? No. When the 12-room house was sold to someone else, did it mean we were not to have volunteers? No. Did many long hours of cleaning, building, and moving mean we should not do this? No. It never entered our minds that we were not supposed to do these things; they were required to help the mountain people. Had we misfocused, confusion could have caused us to interpret our circumstances incorrectly and quit just before God accomplished His will.

> **18. Has God spoken a word to you, but it seems that every-thing has gone wrong?** ◯ Yes ◯ No
> **If so, do your circumstances change God's will?**
> ◯ Yes ◯ No **What should you do?**

The Holy Spirit, who resides in us, reminds us of what the Father is teaching us so that we can confidently proceed with His plans, no matter what the circumstances. Like Joseph, go back to what God said and stake your life on the truth; otherwise, like Jacob, you will mourn because you did not believe God's truth.

Go back to what God said and stake your life on the truth.

Doubt. You may also encounter doubt while you wait on God. A number of times in my (Lonnie's) life when the waiting was confus-ing or long, questions like these arose in my mind: *Did God really say that to me? Is God really doing this? Is God really going to do it? When will I ever see this happen?* I discovered that doubt usually resulted from not seeing things come together in my time frame or in the way I planned it would happen. When the 12-room house was sold to someone else after more than two years of prayer, I immedi-ately began asking God how we had missed His will. In retrospect we hadn't. He had simply not yet completed what He had in mind. However, because God's method didn't fit my expectation, I was tempted to doubt.

Two passages can strengthen your faith by shedding light on the basic nature of doubt. In Mark 11:14,21 Jesus cursed a fig tree, and it withered. Jesus responded to the amazed disciples, "Have faith in God. I assure you: If anyone says to this mountain, 'Be lifted up and thrown into the sea,' and does not doubt in his heart, but believes that what he says will happen, it will be done for him" (Mark 11:22-23). James 1:5-8 says, "If any of you lacks wisdom, he should ask God, who gives to all generously and without criticizing, and it will be given to him. But let him ask in faith without doubting. For the doubter is like the surging sea, driven and tossed by the wind. That person should not expect to receive anything from the Lord. An indecisive man is unstable in all his ways." The meaning of *doubt* in these passages is *to separate one thing from another*. When you doubt, you separate yourself from God's word of truth. When God gives you a promise, you must believe and not doubt that He will bring it to pass.

19. *Doubt* means separating yourself from something.
   What does doubt separate you from?
   ○ Your faith in your ability to believe
   ○ Others' advice   ○ A word from God

Doubt separates you from a word from God. Believing what God says is foundational, and acting on what He says is essential. If you meet those requirements, you will experience the awesome reality of His power demonstrated through you. To ask without doubting, you must be convinced that what God said is true. What could be more convincing than the fact that God said it?

Impatience. What makes you impatient? Sitting in a traffic jam when you are late for a meeting? Seeing what you think needs to be done, but no one is doing it? Not getting what you want when you want it? We get frustrated when events do not match the timetable of our expectations. We want action, and we want it now, so we are inclined to do something to make it happen. In a similar way, we sometimes set a timetable for God. When He seems to drag His feet according

> To ask without doubting, you must be convinced that what God said is true.

to our timetable, we are tempted to make it happen ourselves apart from Him. This motive stems from selfishness, which has no place in God's economy.

When tempted to act prematurely, think about two implications of impatience.

1. Not waiting for God's divine directive implies that we do not believe God really knows what, how, or when things should be done, but we do. When Abraham and Sarah sought a son through Hagar, in effect they tried to bring God's will into being apart from His plan. Their "improvements" didn't work out the way they designed them, to say the least. If we follow their example, we will have their result.

2. Our impatience implies that our knowledge is superior to God's. If God were really wiser than we are, if He actually had knowledge we didn't, and if His plan were truly better than ours, then any rational person would choose His way. When we don't choose it, we declare our plan superior to His.

Recognizing the foolishness of both of these positions helps us remember to trust God and to be faithful while waiting for Him to act.

God cannot bless impatience, because it would shift glory from Him to us. If God recognized our plan over His, if we were allowed to do it our way instead of His way, we would receive credit. But God doesn't share His glory with anyone (see Isa. 48:11). Therefore, we must be vigilant to seek His glory His way, because we can so easily be lured by the world's standards or schemes.

When we were praying about purchasing the hospital, a friend of mine (Lonnie's) wanted to go to the bank and get a loan. After telling him I did not sense that God wanted us to do it that way, I finally consented because of his insistence. We met with the loan officers and began to discuss my finances. Because I don't receive a salary, I could not project my income for the next year. After a lengthy discussion of how God provided for us, the loan officer declared, "Mr. Riley, I would love to help you, but I can't give you a loan based on that!" I replied, "I'm so glad you said that! The only reason I'm here is so that my friend could know God's will for providing for the old hospital building." I knew that God intended to glorify Himself in a different way than taking out a loan, and I wanted my friend to know that God's will did not include going into debt.

"I will act for My own sake, indeed, My own, for how can I be defiled? I will not give My glory to another."
Isaiah 48:11

20. What is the difference between impatient waiting and godly waiting? Mark each statement *T* (true) or *F* (false).

_____ Impatient waiting is using worldly means to attempt to bring about God's will.

_____ Godly waiting is being eager, ready, and poised to act as soon as God shows the next step in fulfilling His word.

_____ Godly waiting results in God's being glorified.

All three statements are true.

Pain or difficulties. Waiting in faith may also cause pain or difficulties that can appear in an almost endless number of different forms. You may experience ridicule from others, as Noah surely experienced while building an ark on dry land. You may see a reduction in finances, a reduced standard of living, an increased workload, or a hectic schedule. You might suffer a period of ill health. God may develop godly qualities in your life by placing difficult people around you. When difficulties arise, your flesh will be tempted to escape them through compromise.

Perhaps the greatest trial occurs when pain is caused by or to loved ones during the waiting period. Family members and friends who have been taught to handle things a certain way may pressure you to give in to their way. Saying no to those you love and respect is painful. Shortly after arriving in Lynch, we had friends come to visit. After seeing the conditions we lived in, they returned to their motel and wept for us. Our time of waiting was painful for them as well.

> Perhaps the greatest trial occurs when pain is caused by or to loved ones during the waiting period.

21. If God led you in an unusual way, what could you say to concerned friends?

_____

_____

You could tell them how God led you to this point. If they understand, you have gained their support. If they do not understand, you do not need to say anything else. They will understand after God brings to pass what He told you. Because of what God has done in Lynch, all those who initially wept for us now rejoice with us.

Comfort zone. Another temptation while waiting on God is the tendency to return to the comfort zone of past experience. God gave a word to the children of Israel that He would deliver them from slavery and would give them a land of their own. However, He took two years preparing them in the desert before leading them to the border of the promised land; then their disobedience delayed their entry for another 38 years. When difficulties and fears arose during that time, the Hebrews longed to return to Egypt. On one occasion they lamented, "Who will feed us meat? We remember the free fish we ate in Egypt, along with the cucumbers, melons, leeks, onions, and garlic. But now our appetite is gone; there's nothing to look at but this manna!" (Num. 11:4-6) How silly! They remembered free fish. Of course it was free; they were slaves! They so longed for a known past experience that they sought to trade it for future freedom.

When faith becomes uncomfortable, we are tempted to return to a comfort zone, to rely on past success for present strategies, or to hesitate accepting a new assignment we have never done before.

When faith becomes uncomfortable, we are tempted to return to a comfort zone.

22. Identify each statement of reliance on past experience as *CZ* (comfort zone), *PS* (past success), or *NA* (new assignment).

___ I feel that God wants me to run for city government to have an impact on our community, but I've never done anything like that before.

___ Ever since I was elected to city government, it's been one headache after another. I'm going to resign and go back to my old job.

___ I know how to do this city-government stuff. It's a breeze. All I have to do this year is what got me here last year.

The answers are *NA, CZ, PS*. Past experiences cannot measure up to the forever-present I AM. Moses gave up all of the pleasures of Egypt to suffer affliction with God's people. He had no reference point for freeing a people; all he had was God, and that was enough. David had no prior experience of kingship; all he had was God, and that was enough. Abraham had no prior experience in sacrificing a son; all he had was God, and that was enough. We had no prior experience in beginning a multifaceted ministry to the mountain people; all we have is God, and that is enough. If you can describe your life in terms other than God, you are not fully in His will. Is God part of what you need or all of what you need?

Is God part of what you need or all of what you need?

23. Check any of the challenges you have faced or are currently facing as you wait on God to give you direction or put the pieces of His plan together. Make notes in the margin about the form these challenges have taken in your life.
○ Confusing circumstances ○ Doubt ○ Impatience
○ Pain or difficulties ○ Comfort zone

Reread the paragraph before the activity. Stop and pray about the challenges you face in waiting for the Lord. Tell Him some ways He is sufficient for your walk of faith.

God Intends Joy During Waiting

James 1:2-3 gives a strange command: "Consider it a great joy, my brothers, whenever you experience various trials, knowing that the testing of your faith produces endurance." These verses connect joy with testing while waiting. How can this be? Does God really expect us to be excited while we experience any of the challenges we have discussed? Is it really possible for a wellspring of faith to bubble up waters of overflowing joy? Absolutely! As Jesus walked daily on this earth, He was continually tested. Yet He constantly rejoiced. In the final 24 hours of His life, He used the word *joy* or *rejoice* eight times. He told His disciples that He wanted them to experience the same joy He had with His Father. God intends for you to be filled with joy even when you are tested.

When your confidence in God's word rises up on wings like eagles, your heart finds renewed strength. When you taste the fruit of anticipation in the middle of your trial, the fulfillment of God's word is sweeter. Can you imagine what David felt during his coronation? What went through the hearts of Sarah and Abraham when Isaac was born? Remember the song that arose from Moses' lips when the children of Israel passed through the Red Sea, but Pharaoh's army perished in it? What do you suppose the disciples experienced at Pentecost? Each one had the profound joy of seeing God fulfill the word He had told them would happen. This is joy indeed!

When I presented an $85,000 cashier's check to the owner of the old hospital and he knew I did not have a single penny one month earlier, the joy I experienced because of the Father's provision was indescribable. The Bible reflects this inverse relationship: the greater the difficulty in waiting, the greater the joy when God brings His word to pass. Waiting can produce immeasurable joy for a Christian who understands and practices the concept of experiencing joy while waiting.

24. On a scale of 1 to 10, how much do you live in anticipation of the rewards and joy that come from doing God's will?

A N T I C I P A T E

1 2 3 4 5 6 7 8 9 10

God who? Well, that's I'm getting it. God will
Life stinks. good for you. come through!

A Walk of Faith

1. _____

2. _____

3. _____

4. _____

5. God rewards completed faith.

We're not talking about a self-serving approach that dangles happiness as the ultimate motivating factor in obeying God. Joy reflects a believer's confidence in Him. If you are completely convinced that God will perform what He has promised, you will be filled with joy. That is the life of faith. It does not mean there will be no difficulties, but our difficulties have purpose as we wait for Him to unveil His will through our lives.

In this chapter we have established that walking by faith requires waiting, waiting requires active seeking, and waiting carries testing. Learning to trust God and wait on Him requires time. Do not be discouraged in the school of faith as the course work goes to a higher level. Expect failures, bumps, and miscues along the way. However, as your faith matures, God will use you more and more. Your life will ever-increasingly become a living demonstration of God's power and glory. In the next chapter we will explore ways God rewards your faith.

25. In the margin write the first four stages in a walk of faith. Look back at previous chapters if you need help.

1. Don Miller, speech, c. 1989.

God Rewards Completed Faith

Have you ever grown a garden? If so, you know that a lot of work is required to produce a good crop. If you want a mouth-watering tomato or a juicy watermelon, you must plow, plant, fertilize, water, weed, and spray. Weeks later the seeds begin pushing through the soil, then grow, blossom, and form fruit. After three long months that sun-ripened tomato finally turns a deep red, and that plump watermelon at last sounds just right when thumped. The fruit matures through a growth process until a day of completion comes.

In the same way, our faith must mature through a process as we walk in a fellowship with God, believe Him when He speaks, respond to Him in faith, and actively seek Him during the waiting stage. Then a day comes when the seed of faith God planted in you arrives at maturity. A farmer's completed labor results in an abundant crop. What results from completed faith? What can you expect the final outcome of faithful, patient obedience to be?

Several times in this study we have examined ways God worked to build the faith of biblical characters. Let's bring these great people of faith to the microphone once again and let them share the results of their walks with God. Brother Noah, what was the outcome of your faith? "The saving of my family and the created order." Father Abraham, what resulted from leaving Ur, sojourning in tents, and offering Isaac to God? "Through me all nations of the earth are blessed, I became the father of faith, and a nation was birthed through which the Messiah came." Moses, what about you? "God delivered my people from slavery, and we became the people of God." Your turn, David. "Through me God established a house that would never end, and Jesus came from my lineage." Jesus, our Lord, what was the outcome of your walk of faith? "I accomplished salvation for humankind, was given the name above every name, and received an eternal kingdom." Brother Paul? "God used me to reveal that His redemptive plan included the Gentiles."

> **1. Which statement accurately reflects the pattern in the lives of these biblical giants?**
> ○ God rewarded every one of them.
> ○ They never saw results from walking by faith.

All Bible characters who obeyed God by faith had one experience in common: God always rewarded them. What about your life? What should you expect to happen after you have done God's will? Will God also reward you? Absolutely! God has incredible blessings in store for all of His children who walk by faith. However, an infinitely wise, eternity-minded Father doesn't necessarily wrap His rewards with the ribbons and bows of our choosing or give them according to our expectations. Their multifaceted, multidimensional characteristics yield some startling surprises.

God has incredible blessings in store for all of His children who walk by faith.

Conditions of God's Rewards

More than 3,100 years ago, a young woman stood on the precipice of a life-altering decision: should she stay in her home country or go to an unknown land with her mother-in-law? We don't know everything that went through Ruth's mind, but part of her decision must have had an element of faith in God, for later in the story Boaz said to her, "May the LORD reward you for what you have done, and may you receive a full reward from the LORD God of Israel, under whose wings you have come for refuge" (Ruth 2:12). Boaz recognized Ruth's act of faith in exchanging the Moabite god Chemosh for the wings of refuge of the Lord God of Israel. He knew she had sacrificed any semblance of a normal, secure, peaceful life in the hometown of her birth to suffer poverty alongside Naomi; therefore, Boaz vocalized a prayer that God would reward her. Did God do that? Did He ever! God immortalized her story by making it a book in the Bible, and from her offspring sprang kings and ultimately the Messiah.

2. **Read Ruth 1:1-18 in your Bible. Put yourself in Ruth's position at the time she left Moab. Which choice best describes her motive for leaving with Naomi?**
   ○ I can't bear to leave Naomi. I'll trust her God to take care of us.
   ○ I knew how it would turn out all along. That's why I left.
   ○ Israel is a happening place. That old woman is my ticket to bigger and better things.

Nobody goes with a penniless widow for personal gain. Obviously, her motive sprang from her love for Naomi. Her story highlights the first of four truths about God's rewards.

Rewards are given to those without ulterior motives. Following God for what a person can receive turns pure motives into cancerous cells of greed. When greed grows unchecked, the tumor of selfishness chokes the spiritual vitality out of a Christian. Anyone in this sickened condition cannot expect anything from God. Simon the sorcerer discovered this truth the hard way. When he saw that the Holy Spirit was given through laying on hands, he offered money to buy this privilege. Peter responded, "You have no part or share in this matter, because your heart is not right before God" (Acts 8:21). Ruth, on the other hand, had no idea she would be a key figure in Jesus' lineage. She did not expect to marry a wealthy man who would take care of her and Naomi; she did not go with her mother-in-law for that purpose. Her sole motive was to serve Naomi.

Following God for what a person can receive turns pure motives into cancerous cells of greed.

3. What about you? What is your motive for walking by faith?
○ Sensationalism. I want to experience the thrill of miracles.
○ Getting a name for myself. I want to be known as spiritual.
○ I want to please God.
○ I want to be a blessing to others.
○ I think it's mixed. God, take out the dross and refine the pure.
○ Other: _____

We do not design or plan the rewards. Ruth did not inform God what her rewards should be, nor did she initiate a plan for obtaining them. When she left Moab, her intention was to eke out a meager living for her and Naomi until death parted them. She did not strategize, *I think I'll get food by gleaning in the fields of Boaz, act virtuous, and inspire him to give me more than enough barley.* She didn't place a conference call to other young widows and discuss how to snag a wealthy husband. She didn't diagram a course of action:

Step 1: Glean in field of rich man. Get noticed.
Step 2: Get permission to keep gleaning in his field. Stay positioned to keep being noticed.
Step 3: Sneak onto threshing floor at barley harvest.
Step 4: Get married. Poverty is history!

When Ruth went to Bethlehem, she didn't even know Boaz existed, much less plan to marry him. She simply responded to what God had placed in her path. She went to work, and God began unveiling His will. We are so trained in strategic planning that we have forgotten about faith. We outline exactly the results we want and the steps we expect God to follow for starting a ministry, giving us a better job, or reaching our community instead of watching for Him to direct our path. When you plan the results of your faith, you have missed faith. When you believe and obey, God brings the results He desires. Ruth married Boaz, and King David's grandfather, Obed, was born. Ruth could not have planned that! In fact, if you can see the final product of faith, if you can plan a desired result, you probably aren't walking by faith. Can you recall a single biblical character who heard from God and planned the results or rewards? Like Abraham and Sarah, some tried, but the result had serious consequences for all future generations. God is quite capable of doing His own planning and letting you know His plan. Then He rewards your walk of faith.

When you plan the results of your faith, you have missed faith.

4. Check the statements that are true.

○ 1. Faith means planning your work and working your plan.

○ 2. If you can outline all of the steps, you aren't walking by faith.

○ 3. Faith is learning the general direction God wants you to go, looking at the opportunity to respond that is before you, then watching Him unfold His will step by step.

○ 4. Faith is sitting around and letting God do everything.

○ 5. God plans your rewards, not you.

Statements 2, 3, and 5 are true. When you walk by faith, God determines the direction, the plan of attack, and the results. I (Lonnie) spent the first 40 years of my life following God according to my own plans. When I returned to Lynch, I could have easily reverted to my old patterns of strategizing the results I wanted and initiating a plan of attack. I could have surveyed what needed to be done, chosen the projects to meet those needs, organized the logistics to make it happen, then picked up the phone and enlisted three hundred volunteers. Instead, my wife and I made a conscious decision to ask God what He wanted. He responded by unveiling His will. First, people in the community began asking us to help; we answered that if God provided, we would obey. We prayed and began watching how God would lead. Next, churches called and requested to come on mission to our area. Then God provided resources for us and increased the impact of the ministry each year. We could not have planned for what is currently happening. More than three thousand volunteers come to Lynch annually, and many people receive Christ. Would you plan for three hundred if God chose to reward you with three thousand? We use the funds God gives us each year. Our budget is whatever He chooses to provide. We do not plan what He may give; we plan to use what He gives. That is responsive planning. Has living without a plan of attack diminished what we might have accomplished otherwise? No! On the contrary. In 2005 we received more than one million dollars in cash, goods, and services. Walking by faith brought rewards we never could have planned.

Walking by faith brought rewards we never could have planned.

We must be content with the type of reward God wishes to give. Generally, we think God rewards faith with things that are pleasing to us. However, do not assume that every reward is physically pleasing. Hebrews 11:33-38 lists ways the faith of the saints generated both pleasant and negative experiences. Some conquered kingdoms, obtained promises, escaped the sword, gained strength, or became mighty in battle. Others, however, were scourged, tortured, afflicted, mistreated, stoned, or sawed in two. In a sense both groups were rewarded, because the results in their lives sprang directly from their obedience of faith.

5. Read Hebrews 11:35-38 in the margin. If you experienced the negative rewards of faith, how would you respond?
○ Is this what I get for serving God?
○ I thought faith might be a challenge, but I never expected anything like this!
○ I must be outside God's will for this to happen.
○ I know this light and temporary affliction is producing eternal glory for me (see 2 Cor. 4:17).
○ The reward of sharing in the fellowship of Jesus' sufferings (see Phil. 3:10) far exceeds the sacrifice of my personal comfort.

"Some men were tortured, not accepting release, so that they might gain a better resurrection, and others experienced mockings and scourgings, as well as bonds and imprisonment. They were stoned, they were sawed in two, they died by the sword, they wandered about in sheepskins, in goatskins, destitute, afflicted, and mistreated. The world was not worthy of them. They wandered in deserts, mountains, caves, and holes in the ground."
Hebrews 11:35-38

Given the perseverance of those saints, they must have adopted an attitude in line with the last two statements. Most likely, they didn't view the troubling rewards of faith as something negative but rather as necessary to receive God's rewards. When people face an unpleasant circumstance in life, it reveals the depth of their faith. Those expecting the rewards of faith to be constantly wonderful, happy, and exciting are in for some disappointments. They will find themselves making statements and asking questions like, Is this what I get for serving God? Such a response shows a lack of understanding about the way God rewards faith. God gives the rewards of faith that will glorify Him. Your expectation, therefore, should be to glorify Him with whatever your reward may be. Look for rewards that are God-honoring, not self-gratifying. When you expect something God didn't intend, you may become discouraged with God. Paul's faith took him through a series of negative situations that could have been devastating, including a shipwreck, stoning, beating, and prison. Were these the result of obedience? Yes, obviously. Paul didn't become disillusioned but declared, "I have learned to be content in whatever circumstances I am" (Phil. 4:11). You must learn to expect only what He wants to give and be content with the results. Until your faith leads you to contentment, it will not take you to another place.

Rewards follow the completion of faith. When did Ruth receive her reward? Was it before or after she did God's will? It was after. She would never have met Boaz if she had stayed in Moab. When did the rewards of faith occur for Shadrach, Meshach, and Abednego? Was it before or after the fire? They had to go through the fire before they experienced God's power to deliver and the promotion of the king. Daniel's act of faith in persevering prayer received no reward until he was lifted out of the lions' den. When did David receive the throne? When He was anointed king? No, after he passed the test of refusing to touch the Lord's anointed. Nowhere in Scripture did God grant a reward on the front end. If He did, no faith would be required, for who believes God for what he already has? Your faith would never grow, and it would be of no value to God. You must first complete what you believe before your faith will be rewarded.

> You must first complete what you believe before your faith will be rewarded.

6. **When God speaks about His will, how should you pray?**
   ○ God, put the provisions in place so that I can do Your will.
   ○ God, show me the first step so that I can begin to do Your will. I know you will provide as the need arises.

We often want God to tell us every detail and outcome before we act or to reassure us by providing ahead of time. He will never do it. A few years ago a couple sensed God leading them to serve with us in Lynch, so I (Lonnie) met with them on several occasions to clarify their call. During one discussion they told me, "God must do certain things before we come." I simply responded, "Then you will never come." When they asked why, I answered, "If you are waiting for God to give you what you need before you believe, then it will not happen." Ultimately, they believed and came; now God has rewarded them by taking care of the details that initially generated their fears.

God rewards completed faith, not those who say they have faith. It is incorrect to say we have faith but not act. No wonder Scripture encourages us, "Don't throw away your confidence, which has a great reward. For you need endurance, so that after you have done God's will, you may receive what was promised" (Heb. 10:35-36). When the fire of testing tempers the steel of faith, God always draws near to strengthen our spirit. In the case of David, God even used Saul on one occasion to prophesy of David's ultimate reward. After

David refused to kill Saul when he had an opportunity to do so, Saul responded, "May the LORD repay you with good for what you have done for me today" (1 Sam. 24:19). He then conceded God's will: "Now I know for certain you will be king, and the kingdom of Israel will be established in your hand" (v. 20). Likewise, when you face testing, God will always encourage you. He who did not withhold His own Son from you graciously desires to give you all things (see Rom. 8:32). However, He will not grant His reward unless your walk of faith meets His standards. God rewards you after your journey of obedience is complete.

> *"He did not even spare His own Son, but offered Him up for us all; how will He not also with Him grant us everything?"*
> Romans 8:32

7. Check the statement that most closely describes your expectation for receiving God's rewards.
  ○ I have been waiting for God to reward my faith. Why haven't I seen His activity in my life?
  ○ I am obediently taking steps of faith, knowing that my reward lies in the future.
  ○ I have failed to act in faith because I have been waiting for God to show me that He approves my faith.

A life of faith means acting in obedience to the steps God directs you to take. Don't expect Him to reward you until your walk of faith is complete.

These four conditions of God's rewards establish our expectations for receiving and appreciating what God wishes to give us. In the remainder of this chapter we will explore the rewards of completed faith, as well as the rewards of incomplete faith.

Rewards of Completed Faith in the Kingdom

In Philippians 4:11 Paul wrote, "I have learned to be content in whatever circumstances I am." How did Paul learn contentment? How could he possibly find wisdom in weakness, calm in catastrophe, and peace in pressure? How could his lips utter, "I am pleased in weaknesses, in insults, in catastrophes, in persecutions, and in pressures" (2 Cor. 12:10)? If his life had revolved around self-actualization, he could not have been content in these circumstances, but Paul found meaning in a life molded by other motives.

8. What were the motives that molded Paul's life?

That God be _____

That the church be _____

That humanity be _____

Any number of answers could be correct. The three we chose relate to Christ's desire for His kingdom. They are: God is glorified, the church is edified, and humanity is redeemed. Each of these goals is a reward of completed faith in God's kingdom.

God is glorified. When God works through your faith, others respond to Him. Scripture reveals that one of the most common responses to the display of divine power is the glorification of God. For example, in Mark 2 when Jesus returned to His home in Capernaum, word quickly spread throughout the town. Immediately, the house filled with so many people that no one could even enter the door. Four undeterred friends of a paralytic devised an ingenious way to grab Jesus' attention. They carried their friend onto the rooftop, tore off the tiles, and lowered him into the Lord's presence. When Jesus witnessed their faith, He healed the man, who promptly arose, took up his bed, and walked out in plain sight of the slack-jawed onlookers. Verse 12 highlights the reaction: "They were all astounded and gave glory to God, saying, 'We have never seen anything like this!'"

In Acts 3 a man lame from birth sat at the temple gate begging for alms. Peter fixed his attention on him and declared, "I have neither silver nor gold, but what I have, I give to you: In the name of Jesus Christ the Nazarene, get up and walk!" (Acts 3:6). The man's ankle bones were strengthened, and he immediately entered the temple complex "walking, leaping, and praising God" (v. 8).

These two examples show that glorifying God is the end result of faith that is put into action. In fact, at least 13 times the Gospels link the glorification of God to someone's actions (see Matt. 9:8; 15:31; Mark 2:12; Luke 4:15; 5:26; 7:16; 13:13; 17:15; 23:47; John 11:4; 14:13; 15:8; 17:4). No wonder Jesus encouraged us in the Sermon on the Mount to "let your light shine before men, so that they may see your good works and give glory to your Father in

> When God works through your faith, others respond to Him.

heaven" (Matt. 5:16). People glorify God most when they see God working through us. This explains why God gave a baby to a 90-year-old woman, reduced Gideon's army from 32,000 to 300, and let a boy kill a giant. Their lives became living examples that glorified God.

9. How would you describe the way your life is glorifying God?

_____

_____

Unfortunately, many believers today seek to follow God with no-faith-required works, producing no-glory-gained results. What we accomplish can usually be explained in terms of how we did it instead of how God did it. If anything good happens, those watching often misplace the glory by crediting us with the results.

The principle of misplaced glory also results from misplaced faith. Paul warned the new Christians to be on guard against those who would compromise their foundation: "I am saying this so that no one will deceive you with persuasive arguments. Be careful that no one takes you captive through philosophy and empty deceit based on human tradition, based on the elemental forces of the world, and not based on Christ" (Col. 2:4,8). These young Christians were learning that faith could be easily misplaced if we do not keep in focus the fact that "it is God who is working in you, enabling you both to will and to act for *His* good purpose" (Phil. 2:13, emphasis added). Faith is all about God—His person, His plan, His power, and His purpose. Philosophy (thinking patterns or beliefs) that is not of God can breed traditions that are good but are not God's. From these traditions sprout world-centered principles rather than godly principles. By following the world's ways, we move farther and farther from walking by faith and closer and closer to walking by sight.

Perhaps no other group found themselves more thoroughly ensnared in this trap than the Pharisees. Originally, they had started with the best intentions, but over time they became so tradition-bound that Jesus lamented in Mark 7:6-9, "These people honor Me with their lips, but their heart is far from Me. They worship Me in vain, teaching as doctrines the commands of men. Disregarding the command of God, you keep the tradition of men. ... You completely

> Many believers today seek to follow God with no-faith-required works, producing no-glory-gained results.

invalidate God's command in order to maintain your tradition!" Somewhere along the way, the Pharisees' minds were captured by vain thinking patterns, beliefs, and philosophies; that mentality bred traditions in conflict with God's Word. So confident were they in their traditions, however, that they looked to them to interpret God's Word. Their misplaced faith deceived them, rendering the entirety of their existence of no spiritual value. Nothing of God's glory shone through them. Little wonder Paul admonished the Colossian Christians to let no one deceive them by vain philosophies or traditions!

10. What are some thinking patterns, beliefs, philosophies, or traditions that may limit faith today?

_____

_____

Some stumbling blocks to faith include doing what you know how to do instead of what God said to do, setting a goal for what you want your faith to produce, doing something for God that will make you more important or give you a big name, or demanding that a church service be conducted a certain way.

The church is edified. We can trace another reward of completed faith in the Book of Acts. Several times Luke's account included statements such as "The church throughout all Judea, Galilee, and Samaria had peace, being built up" (9:31), "strengthening the hearts of the disciples by encouraging them" (14:22), "encouraged the brothers and strengthened them" (15:32), "strengthening the churches" (v. 41), "The churches were strengthened in the faith" (16:5), and "strengthening all the disciples" (18:23). All of these phrases follow someone's obedience in doing God's will. Stephen's prayer of forgiveness and Ananias's laying hands on Paul tremendously strengthened the early church. Paul and Barnabas's obedience to the Holy Spirit's call on their lives resulted in church plants and the building up of those churches. The Jerusalem Council's wise decision greatly encouraged the Gentile churches in the faith. In every instance God rewarded the faith of these individuals by strengthening the church.

God rewarded the faith of these individuals by strengthening the church.

I (Lonnie) have seen this pattern repeated multiple times in mission teams. One church from South Carolina stands out in particular. During its week of ministry with us, God began powerfully inspiring members' hearts to serve at home in the same manner as they had on the mission trip. He then opened their eyes to the opportunities He was presenting them in their state. This group went back home and started six new ministries. God rewarded their initial step of completed faith by edifying them to walk with Him in new ways. Anytime God's people experience God working in ways that can be explained only in terms of Him, they are tremendously edified. A congregation could be in the most abysmal circumstances, devoid of any outward reasons for hope; yet members' hearts would soar as God did the unexplainable through them.

A few years ago the Lord gave us an empty church building. Sensing that God wanted to revive a church there and use the building more than two days a week, we sought Him to learn what the next step should be. Shortly, another church called and asked if we could use some dental equipment. There it was! Now during the week we have two complete dental offices in the church building, including X-ray machines. Later that ministry expanded to optometry equipment and free medical exams. As a result, a new church has been started there, the members have been strengthened, and many people have come to Christ.

11. Which of the following are ways a church can be edified?
   ○ People are saved.
   ○ New ministries are begun.
   ○ Things happen that can be attributed only to God.
   ○ Other churches are encouraged and motivated.

God rewards a congregation that lets Him plan the work and works the plan His way.

A church can be edified in all of these ways. God rewards a congregation that lets Him plan the work and works the plan His way. He fills any people who trust Him exclusively and honor Him publicly. When a church is edified, even the community takes on a new spirit.

Humanity is redeemed. Another reward of faith in God's kingdom is that people are redeemed. When God composed the music of Scripture, He wrote a certain melody line throughout the score. Jesus believed His Father, and atonement for humanity was made possible.

Peter and others fearlessly preached on the day of Pentecost, and three thousand were added to the church. The new converts sold their possessions to meet others' needs, and people were added daily to the church. Philip trusted God enough to go to a desert road, and the Ethiopian eunuch came to Christ. Peter went with Gentiles, and Cornelius and his household were saved. Paul and Barnabas went on a missionary journey, and people turned to the Lord. The music score of Acts reveals this truth: God is always in the process of redeeming humanity through the completed faith of those who obey Him. In each example others came to know God after a Christian obeyed God. No one became converted first, then tracked down a believer for church membership. A Christian responded in faith before the conversion of others resulted. If you walk by sight and not by faith, you will miss the opportunity to see God's miraculous work of salvation. If you slip into a comfort zone or shrink back from God's leading, His truth will not be manifested through you, and those who are watching will not see God and be drawn to Him. When we allow God to order our steps and He does something through us, His Spirit bears witness of the truth of His Son to a lost world.

I (John) once met a doctor to whom God had spoken about two things. First, he needed to gain a heart for the lost. Second, if he would make his love for the Lord his priority in prayer, God would provide opportunities for witnessing. As the doctor obeyed in faith, God redeemed about 125 people in his office over a two-year period.

> God is always in the process of redeeming humanity through the completed faith of those who obey Him.

12. Mark each statement *T* for *true* or *F* for *false*.

___ When we obey, God demonstrates Himself to others.

___ Others are redeemed before we respond in faith to God.

___ Because God wishes to redeem, you should always watch for persons God is drawing to Himself.

Recall the three rewards of completed faith in the kingdom.

God is _____ .

The church is _____ .

Humanity is _____ .

You probably answered *T, F, T.* As you walk in faith, watch for persons God is drawing to Himself. He can use you to reach them if you are obedient. The three rewards of completed faith in God's kingdom are: God is glorified, the church is edified, and humanity is redeemed. Now let's look at the rewards of completed faith in you.

Rewards of Completed Faith in You

God has an uncanny ability not only to advance His kingdom through your completed faith but also to simultaneously work in you every good thing He desires for your life. Your praying, waiting, watching, and acting will be crowned with unspeakable joy. Your soul will be aflame with the desire to experience Him time and time again. God will give you good things—the blessing of participation, the reality of God's promise, joy and strength to continue living by faith, and a deeper walk of faith.

The blessing of participation. The Apostle Paul made an unusual assumption about the nature of faith in Ephesians 2:8-10. In verses 8-9 he taught that we are "saved through faith ... not from works." However, the next verse explains the foundation of salvation by grace, not works: "For we are His creation—created in Christ Jesus for *good works,* which God prepared ahead of time so that we should walk in them" (v. 10, emphasis added). Did you catch the paradox? We are not saved by good works, but the moment we are saved, God assigns us good works! Therefore, it is spiritually impossible to be saved and then do nothing. In fact, in 15 verses the Bible specifically uses the phrase *good works.* Not once is the phrase used in a negative sense, and a number of verses actually command us to do them (see Matt. 5:16; John 10:32; Acts 9:36; Rom. 13:3; Eph. 2:10; 1 Tim. 2:10; 5:10,25; 6:18; Titus 2:7,14; 3:8,14; Heb. 10:24; 1 Pet. 2:12).

> It is spiritually impossible to be saved and then do nothing.

13. Why do you think God strongly emphasizes good works?
- ○ 1. God can't get all of His work done and needs our help.
- ○ 2. The nature of faith requires participation with God.
- ○ 3. We don't become saved by good works, but we stay saved by good works.
- ○ 4. You're overstating it. Good works aren't that big a deal.

The answer is 2. Paul assumed that the nature of faith requires participation with God—the participation of walking in good works that God has prepared ahead of time, not that we should do them but walk in them. Both of the phrases *ahead of time* and *walk in them* suggest God has already done the work and we merely participate with Him. Does He involve us because He needs us? No, He involves us because He has designed everything we experience of Him after salvation to come through participating with Him by faith. All great people of faith in the Bible, throughout history, and today have considered experiencing God's presence as they participated with Him their greatest reward. As you learn to walk by faith, you will increasingly count the blessing of participation with God your greatest reward as well.

In 1999 when God instructed Belinda and me (Lonnie) to return to Lynch, He told us that we would not have a fancy home or large salaries, but we would have Him. We initially made sacrifices, but years later we would not trade one former possession for the indescribable joy of participating in God's work. We are constantly amazed at what God can do right where we are. Now we understand Paul when he said, "I also count all things loss for the excellence of the knowledge of Christ Jesus my Lord, for whom I have suffered the loss of all things, and count them as rubbish, that I may gain Christ" (Phil. 3:8, NKJV). This reward of knowing God more deeply by participating with Him is the greatest blessing a believer can experience.

The reality of God's promise. Do you think it odd that Moses, when he looked back over the Red Sea and saw Pharaoh's army destroyed, broke out in jubilant song? Of course not, for the Israelites had just received the reality of what God had promised—freedom from Egyptian bondage. Do you think it odd that Mary spontaneously burst into praise when Gabriel announced that she would bear the Messiah? No, because she believed the reality of the promise would come to pass. Do you think it strange that in the fleeting moments of Stephen's life, he died with courage? Obviously not, for he saw Jesus standing at the right hand of God, ready to make His promise to receive him a reality. Faith is believing in the reality of what God has promised.

> Faith is believing in the reality of what God has promised.

14. In these examples when did the reality of God's promise occur that caused rejoicing?
○ The reality of God's promise occurred after they rejoiced.
○ The reality of God's promise occurred; then Moses rejoiced. Mary rejoiced; then it occurred later. Stephen rejoiced as it occurred.
○ The reality of God's promise occurred before they rejoiced.

The moment God promises is the moment reality occurs, regardless of when we rejoice. When God told Mary, it was as good as done. For Stephen the reality of heaven occurred long before His stoning. God told Moses months earlier that deliverance would come.

If you receive a promise from God, that is all the reality you need. Hebrews 11:13 spotlights this truth in the lives of some Old Testament characters: "These all died in faith without having received the promises, but they saw them from a distance, greeted them, and confessed that they were foreigners and temporary residents on the earth." Reality occurred when they saw the promises, not at the moment the promises were fulfilled. That's why after being "warned about what was not yet seen" (v. 7), Noah immediately began building an ark. "Faith is the reality of what is hoped for, the proof of what is not seen" (v. 1). When you believe what you cannot see, then what you believe will be seen. When you embrace the promise, you possess it, perhaps not with your hand but with your heart. What God puts in your heart will sooner or later come to your hand. In every instance in the Bible, God rewarded someone by making the invisible reality visible. Walking by faith allows you to live in the certainty of God's reality.

We moved to southeast Kentucky because God gave us a promise from Isaiah 41:17-20 of what He intended to do. God used that passage to give us this promise: "The poor and needy seek water, but there is none; their tongues are parched with thirst. I, the Lord, will answer them; I, the God of Israel, do not forsake them. I will open rivers on the barren heights and springs in the middle of the plains … so that all may see and know, consider and understand, that the hand of the Lord has done this." Just as God heard the cry of His people in Egypt, He had heard the cry of people in the mountains. The past seven years have demonstrated that God's word to us is true (see 2 Cor. 1:20). What an incredible God!

"Every one of God's promises is 'Yes' in Him. Therefore the 'Amen' is also through Him for God's glory through us."
2 Corinthians 1:20

140

15. Is the following statement true or false?
When God gives you a promise of what He will do, He will one day make it visible. **Circle your answer:** True   False

What reality has God brought into your life that He is waiting for you to believe?

_____

The statement is true. The reality is born when God makes the promise. You can believe it.

Joy and strength to continue. God made nothing in creation to be inherently self-sustaining. Every living creature grows weak and needs renewed strength. Nehemiah 8:10 reveals that God has designed strength to come from joy: "Your strength comes from rejoicing in the LORD." If you have joy in what you do, you will also have the strength you need. When joy subsides, you are weak, and tasks become drudgery. However, when God moves again, your joy is restored, and your strength blossoms anew like a flower in springtime. You can then believe God more and more. One reward of faith is that God increasingly renews your joy and strength to continue in His service, so that Psalm 100:2 becomes your daily reality:

> *Serve the LORD with gladness;*
> *come before Him with joyful songs.*

Joy and gladness are the defining qualities of a life lived by faith. Why? The next verse provides the answer: "Acknowledge that the LORD is God" (Ps. 100:3). When we know by faith that the Lord is God, we have joy and strength in serving Him.

Joy and gladness are the defining qualities of a life lived by faith.

16. On a scale of 1 to 10, what is your joy quotient?

1	2	3	4	5	6	7	8	9	10
Low									High

A deeper walk of faith. God's work always moves from small to large; therefore, do not expect Him to display His earth-changing power initially. Many Christians err by looking for big things and are disappointed when they do not come. Moses merely saw a burning bush that was not consumed—a bit out of the ordinary but not earth-changing. Yet Moses' simple response to what he saw of God became a mighty movement of God. Paul's encounter with the Lord on the road to Damascus was not earth-changing, but his initial response of faith became the avenue through which God would bring the gospel to the Gentiles. When we respond in faith to little things, God's work increases in our lives. When His work increases, our faith likewise grows. A deeper walk of faith is one of the greatest rewards of faith.

God taught this lesson to Belinda and me (Lonnie) when we first returned to Lynch. The economic condition and population exodus had left the town in disarray. A number of neglected, vacant homes with untrimmed hedges lined the streets. Not knowing what else to do, I bought a set of hedge clippers for $24.99 and for several days went up and down the street trimming hedges. About that time a man stopped by the house and asked, "Could you spare $75? My family hasn't eaten well in days." "I don't have $75," I replied, "but if the Lord gives it to me, I'll give it to you." Two days later I was outside when a woman from a neighboring state pulled into the driveway and announced that she had come to pay her bill. I answered her, "You don't owe me anything, Ma'am. In fact, I've never even seen you before." "Are you the one who's been cutting everyone's hedges?" she inquired. "Yes, but I was doing it because God sent me here, not because I was trying to earn money." "Well, I own the house two doors over. I always pay to have my hedges cut, and you did a good job. I'm going to pay you," she stated rather matter-of-factly. Then she laid down a $100 bill and declared, "If you do not pick it up, it will lie there."

You don't have to say that twice to a broke preacher in southeast Kentucky! I picked it up and decided to celebrate at the local steakhouse that night, but God whispered to my heart, "You told that man you would give him $75 if I gave it to you." With joy I immediately called the gentleman and announced, "You can come down and pick up the $75 God has just provided for you. And when you sit down tonight to a warm meal for the first time in a long time, realize that God has been immeasurably good to you." As I gave him the money, the Lord spoke again to my heart, "Not only did I give him $75, but I also repaid you for the $24.99 hedge clippers!"

> When we respond in faith to little things, God's work increases in our lives.

This wonderful lesson set the precedent for other times of trusting God. We learned that God typically asks us to follow Him in simple ways. When we obey in the little things, He strengthens our faith so that we can believe Him for much larger things. That act of small obedience eventually resulted in thousands making professions of faith, communities being rebuilt, and God being glorified!

17. List simple things God has done to strengthen your faith.

God's Act	How It Strengthened Faith
_____	_____
_____	_____
_____	_____

Check the rewards of completed faith you have experienced in your life.
○ The blessing of participation   ○ The reality of God's promise
○ Joy and strength to continue   ○ A deeper walk of faith

Rewards of Incomplete Faith

After we are saved, our walk of faith determines the rewards we will receive at the time of judgment. God's Word warns us of the consequences of incomplete faith (see Heb. 10:35-38 ; 2 John 8).

God is not pleased. Hebrews 10:38 states God's response to someone who starts by faith but does not complete it:

> *My righteous one will live by faith;*
> *and if he draws back,*
> *My soul has no pleasure in him.*

Evidently, some had started walking by faith but drew back. The writer warned them of the result of that course of action: God's very soul would have no pleasure in them! Can you imagine anything more devastating on the day of judgment than to hear others receive the commendation "Well done, good and faithful slave! You were faithful over a few things; I will put you in charge of many things.

"Don't throw away your confidence, which has a great reward. For you need endurance, so that after you have done God's will, you may receive what was promised. For in yet a very little while, the Coming One will come and not delay. But My righteous one will live by faith; and if he draws back, My soul has no pleasure in him."
Hebrews 10:35-38

"Watch yourselves so that you don't lose what we have worked for, but you may receive a full reward."
2 John 8

Share your master's joy!" (Matt. 25:23), while the Lord withholds the same praise from you? May none of us receive this reward.

We will not receive the reward. Just before the sobering warning in Hebrews 10:38, verses 35-36 encourage us, "Don't throw away your confidence, which has a great reward. For you need endurance, so that after you have done God's will, you may receive what was promised." This exhortation teaches that if our faith is completed, we have a great reward. If our faith is incomplete, we lose the reward. If we do not believe God along the course of life, we will not see Him demonstrate His power through us to impact our generation. Perhaps the greatest sorrow we will experience on the day of judgment is the awareness of the reward we would have received if we had persevered in faith. May none of us receive this reward.

18. In what areas of your life do you especially need help in walking by faith?

_____

_____

Others' faith will be adversely affected. Being a Christian implies that you are an example or a standard of faith. Those watching you will form conclusions about faith based on the standard you set, whether good or bad. Paul wrote in Philippians 1:12-14 that as a result of his imprisonment, Christ was made known to the imperial guard, and other Christians were emboldened by his example to speak the gospel more fearlessly. When people saw God through Paul's faith, his standard created a thirst for God to move powerfully in their lives. When people do not see God working through us, the standard we set is that our message is irrelevant.

Do not try to take Jesus as an add-on to your life. He *is* your life! Do not ask Him to forgive all your sins and straighten out everything unpleasant without touching things you like. Don't ask Him to fix all of your problems while declaring your home, automobile, lifestyle choices, and leisuretime activities off limits to Him. A life of faith means allowing Christ to live through you and responding to Him in obedience, not getting a ticket to heaven and continuing to

"I want you to know, brothers, that what has happened to me has actually resulted in the advancement of the gospel, so that it has become known throughout the whole imperial guard, and to everyone else, that my imprisonment is for Christ. Most of the brothers in the Lord have gained confidence from my imprisonment and dare even more to speak the message fearlessly."
Philippians 1:12-14

do things your way. A legacy of incomplete faith will cause many to reject the gospel and will weaken the faith of other Christians. May none of us receive this reward.

19. Fill in the blanks to complete the rewards of incomplete faith.

God is not _____ .

We will not _____ the reward.

Others' faith will be _____ affected.

Stop and pray about whether these warnings apply to your walk of faith. What actions do you need to take in light of these warnings?

_____

_____

Faith Is Open-Ended

In this study we have concentrated on two primary truths about faith:
1. The relational nature of a faith walk with God
2. How to respond to God in faith as He accomplishes His will through you

These truths indicate the open-ended nature of faith. Our walk of faith doesn't end when God fulfills His word to you. God always moves you from faith to faith (see Rom. 1:17). When you complete one step of faith, it leads to others, each step becoming a foundation on which God increases opportunities and assignments. For example, David's life moved from sheep, to Goliath, to military victories, to king over one tribe, to king over all Israel, to the lineage of the Messiah. Paul moved from the Damascus road, to working with Gentiles in Antioch, to various missionary journeys, to writing Scripture. God's work builds on itself. Likewise, as you continue to

"God's righteousness is revealed from faith to faith, just as it is written: The righteous will live by faith."
Romans 1:17

walk by faith, you will gain new opportunities to do God's will. If you obey Him today, tomorrow, and the next day, the sum total of these days will bring you to complete fulfillment of His will for your life. God will take you into arenas you never dreamed of, and your life will become a thread with which God can weave a beautiful tapestry of His love for your generation. When Paul admonished the saints at Philippi to "work out your own salvation with fear and trembling" (Phil. 2:12), he meant for believers to fully complete by faith all that God has in mind for our lives. We accomplish this as we walk in an open-ended journey of faith, obeying each step along the way.

God has designed your life to be incredibly significant, and He will unveil what He has in mind for you as you walk with Him by faith. He has hidden, inexpressible joys to reveal along the path of faith if you are willing to obey. Has He awakened a hunger in you to see Him move mightily where you are? Is your heart crying out to experience more of Him? Has He placed that yearning in your soul because He is inviting you to go with Him? Could God intend to make Himself known through you to hundreds where you are? Does He want you to experience all He intended when He saved you? Our prayer is that you will use the biblical patterns and personal examples in this study to strengthen your faith walk with God. May God use your life as a visible demonstration of the rich blessings that come to those who trust Him with reckless abandon and live the adventure of faith. May God ever-increasingly change lives through your growing knowledge of and obedience to Him.

20. In the margin try listing from memory the five stages in a walk of faith. If you need help, see pages 23–27.

What is the next step you need to take in your walk of faith?

_____

_____

_____

A Walk of Faith

1. _____
   _____
   _____ .

2. _____
   _____
   _____ .

3. _____
   _____
   _____ .

4. _____
   _____
   _____ .

5. _____
   _____
   _____ .

Leader Guide

By Faith: Living in the Certainty of God's Reality explores the biblical meaning of faith and challenges members to live by faith. After completing this study, group members will be able to—

- explain why God expects believers to live by faith;
- describe what it means to live by faith;
- give examples of biblical characters who walked by faith;
- name five stages through which God develops a walk of faith;
- outline a four-step process God uses to accomplish His will through believers' faith response;
- explain how to wait on God;
- identify the rewards of completed faith.

This leader guide will help you facilitate six group sessions of 1 to 1½ hours each.

Session 1
The Normal Christian Life

Learning Goals

After the session members will be able to—

- explain why God expects believers to live by faith;
- cite evidence indicating that the normal Christian life is a life of faith;
- identify three proofs of God's desire to have a faith relationship with His children;
- name five stages in a life of faith.

Before the Session

1. Study chapter 1. Complete the activities.
2. Ask members to bring their high-school yearbooks. Or make a montage of pictures depicting fashions in the 1950s, '60s, '70s, '80s, and '90s.
3. Prepare the following assignment slips.
   - *Group 1:* Read Matthew 8:23-25; 10:7-8; 22:15; 15:32-33; 17:27; 21:2; Mark 1:17; John 21:6. Identify ways Jesus began training His disciples in faith as soon as He called them.
   - *Group 2:* Read Matthew 8:10,23-25; 9:22; 14:29-30; 15:28; 17:19-20; 21:19. Identify ways Jesus connected His work in and through His disciples' lives to their faith.
   - *Group 3:* Read Matthew 6:30; 8:26; 13:57-58; 16:8. Identify ways Jesus showed His displeasure when His disciples did not exhibit faith.
4. Have large sheets of paper, markers, and masking tape for group work.
5. Create a handout by listing the following questions and leaving space for responses. Make a copy for each member.

How Is God Building a Faith Relationship with You?

- What has God brought or allowed in your life to train you to walk by faith?
- What are some ways God has connected His work in your life to your faith?
- How has God shown His pleasure or displeasure with your faith?

6. Make handouts with these points.

Stages in a Walk of Faith
- God _____ a faith relationship.
- God develops _____ for a consistent walk of faith.
- God requires a _____ _____ to the unveiling of His will.
- God matures faith through _____.
- God _____ completed faith.

7. Prepare a poster with the heading *Stages in a Walk of Faith* and the five stages: *1. God initiates a faith relationship. 2. God develops fellowship for a consistent walk of faith. 3. God requires a faith response to the unveiling of His will. 4. God matures faith through waiting. 5. God rewards completed faith.*
8. Be prepared to overview the five stages in "Living by Faith" in chapter 1 (p. 22).

During the Session

1. Have members examine fashions in their high-school yearbooks or in the montage you prepared. Ask: *If your style was once normal, would it be abnormal now? How could normal then be abnormal now? If you flipped through God's yearbook of the Old Testament, how would you describe normal? Does God's idea of normal change as our fashions do?*
2. Ask members to scan Hebrews 11 and to identify the number of times the phrase *by faith* and a person's name appear together. Write the names on a dry-erase board. Add New Testament figures such as Jesus, Peter, and Paul. Ask for examples from history, such as George Mueller and Corrie ten Boom. Ask: *What does this evidence imply about God's desire for your life?* Explain: *A lifestyle of faith is the standard for a normal walk with God in the Bible, in history, and today.*
3. Ask: *On a scale of 1 to 10, how intensely do you think God desires a faith walk?* Say: *We can answer that by examining ways Jesus taught the disciples to walk by faith.* Divide members into three groups and give each group one of the assignment slips you prepared, along with a large sheet of paper, a marker, and masking tape. Ask groups to read the Scriptures and to record and display ways Jesus trained the disciples to walk by faith. Possible answers:
- *Group 1:* Gave them an assignment bigger than themselves (become fishers of men, go on missionary journey, cast out demons), led them into problems (storm on Sea of Galilee, opposition from Pharisees, a desert place with no bread), gave them obedience commands (go catch a fish, and you will find a coin; go get a donkey; cast your net on the right side of the boat).
- *Group 2:* Used teaching points (storm on Sea of Galilee, fig tree that withered, explaining why they couldn't cast out a demon), used others' examples (centurion, Bartimaeus, woman with issue of blood, Syrophonecian woman), gave rebukes ("you of little faith" statements, Peter sinking in the water).
- *Group 3:* Their inability to cast out a demon, "you of little faith" statements, few miracles in His hometown.

4. From the disciples' pattern, show members that walking by faith is a lifestyle that God desires for each of us. The way He guides us to walk by faith may vary. For some faith is required in finances; for others faith means stepping into an arena beyond our comfort zone; others must put themselves in a position for God to use them to change others. Yet the common denominator is that doing God's will requires faith.

5. Explain: *God connects His work in and through our lives to our faith. This is especially true for our prayer lives.* Ask three members to read aloud Matthew 21:22; Mark 11:24; and James 1:5-7. Summarize: *Receiving answers to prayer from God requires faith.*

6. Read aloud Hebrews 11:6. State: *Refusing to believe God calls His character, power, and faithfulness into question, implying that He either can't or won't come through.*

7. Distribute copies of the handout "How Is God Building a Faith Relationship with You?" Ask members to work in pairs to answer the questions. Urge them to refer to the handouts at home as they talk with God about their faith walk.

8. Explain: *The goal of this study is to learn how to walk with God by faith.* Distribute copies of the handout "Stages in a Walk of Faith" and ask members to fill in the blanks as you overview the five stages of faith to be covered in this study. Display the poster with the five stages and assure members that they can learn to walk by faith as the biblical giants did.

Session 2
God Initiates a Faith Relationship

Learning Goals

After the session members will be able to—
- explain how God initiates a faith relationship through radical intersection;
- identify the correct response to God's radical intersection of our lives;
- explain why faith is relational in nature;
- distinguish among three definitions of *faith;*
- cite errors in Word of Faith theology.

Before the Session

1. Study chapter 2. Complete the activities.
2. Make three placards: *God first turns the person's attention to Himself. God leads the person toward a defining moment that requires a response. In a defining moment God leads the person to salvation by faith.* Be prepared to summarize these points from "God Radically Intersects a Lost Person's Life" (pp. 33–38).
3. Enlist three members to summarize the points in "What Happens When God Intersects Our Lives?" (pp. 40–44).
4. Bring a piece of asphalt or concrete.
5. Enlist a member to report on the beliefs and errors of Word of Faith theology, based on "Does Faith Mean We Can Name It and Claim It?" (pp. 50–51).
6. Display the poster "Stages in a Walk of Faith," used in session 1.

During the Session

1. State that a lot of opinions exist about faith. Read aloud the following quotations: "Faith is something you believe

that nobody in his right mind would believe."[1] "Faith in one's self … is the best and safest course."[2] "Look into Jesus' Eyes. Then go and be alone and kneel on this Rug of Faith or touch it to both knees. Then please check your needs on our letter to you."[3] "We acknowledge that the crucifixion of Jesus and his resurrection served to uplift faith to understand eternal life, even the allness of Soul, Spirit, and the nothingness of matter."[4] The tongue "can kill you, or it can release the life of God within you." This is so because "faith is a seed. … You plant it by speaking it."[5] "We have not lost faith, but we have transferred it from God to the medical profession."[6]

2. Ask rhetorically: *What is your expectation for the way God will lead you by faith?* Display the poster "Stages in a Walk of Faith" and state that this session will explore stage 1: *God initiates a faith relationship.* State: *God often dramatically intersects lives to initiate a faith relationship.* Ask the group to define *radical intersection* (see p. 30). Call for biblical examples. Ask if volunteers would like to give testimonies of how this happened to them. Use the illustration of the potter waking up the clay, pages 32–33, to show why God radically intersects lives in this manner.

3. Show the three placards you prepared as you explain and give biblical examples of the ways God awakens a person to a life of faith.

4. State: *Sometimes God must also radically intersect a saved person's life when that person has become unresponsive to God.* Cite the examples of David, Jonah, and Peter on page 39. Ask if a volunteer would like to share a time when God radically intersected his life to redirect his walk of faith.

5. State: *John Newton was a slave trader who rejected God. After God radically intersected his life and saved him, his awareness of his unworthiness led him to write "Amazing Grace."* Use the line "that saved a wretch like me" to emphasize that salvation is by faith alone, not by works. Ask three members to read aloud Romans 5:1-2; Galatians 3:10-14; and Ephesians 2:8-9.

6. State: *Some people respond in faith to God's radical intersection, while others do not.* Make two columns on a dry-erase board labeled *Responded Correctly* and *Responded Incorrectly.* Ask the group to brainstorm biblical characters in each category as you list them. *Correctly:* Abraham, Jacob, Joseph, Rahab, Gideon, Paul, David, Hezekiah, Josiah, 11 of the 12 disciples, many people in the New Testament. *Incorrectly:* Pharaoh, Balaam, Saul, Judas, Pharisees, rich young man, Felix.

7. Ask: *Why did these characters respond differently to God's work?* Say: *Some practiced three truths when God radically intersected their lives: (1) Focus on God instead of self. (2) Surrender your desires to God's desires. (3) Become teachable. These are ways believers become or remain pliable clay in God's hands.* Call on the members enlisted to summarize these three points.

8. Ask: *Why could the great saints respond according to these truths, but others could not?* Show the asphalt or concrete and explain that they had the right foundation in their lives—a relationship with God. Ask a member to read aloud the paragraph beginning, "Jesus did not want the disciples to have faith in something but in Someone," page 45.

9. Ask if anyone can recall the three definitions of *faith* (p. 46). Assign the following verses to be read aloud. Ask the group to identify which definition they illustrate: Matthew 8:10 (relationship of trust in God), Jude 3 (beliefs), Acts 15:9 (mode of salvation), Ephesians 2:8 (mode of salvation), Hebrews 11:7 (relationship of trust in God), Acts 6:7 (beliefs), Romans 4:13 (mode of salvation), Acts 14:9 (relationship of trust in God), Galatians 1:23 (beliefs), James 1:6 (relationship of trust in God). Ask: *What percentage of your Christian teaching has centered on faith as a belief system? On faith as a relationship? What is the difference between trusting in a concept and trusting a Person?*

10. Call on the member enlisted to report on the beliefs and errors of Word of Faith theology. Ask members to name TV personalities who teach these errors. Ask: *What do you think is the appeal of these teachings? Do these people focus on a relationship or a formula?* Challenge members to place their faith in God, not in their own faith, and to position themselves to hear a word of truth from Him instead of mustering a word that comes from personal desires.

Session 3
God Develops Fellowship for a Consistent Walk of Faith

Learning Goals
After the session members will be able to—
- identify ways God uses life experiences to train them to walk by faith;
- explain why God guides believers only through maintained fellowship;
- outline a three-step process God uses to develop fellowship with Him;
- identify changes needed to walk by faith;
- name six qualities that result from maintained fellowship with God.

Before the Session
1. Study chapter 3. Complete the activities.
2. Enlist six members to describe the six qualities in "Practicing Fellowship with God" in chapter 3 (pp. 69–75).
3. Set up a simple obstacle course in the room. Bring a blindfold to the session.
4. Display the poster "Stages in a Walk of Faith," used in previous sessions.

During the Session
1. Point to the poster "Stages in a Walk of Faith" and state: *In the second stage God develops in us the understanding and habits we need to walk by faith. He does this by teaching us to maintain fellowship with Him, that is, to keep our relationship with Him in good standing.* Use the examples of David, Joseph, and the disciples (pp. 54–56).
2. Enlist a volunteer to navigate the obstacle course. Then announce that he or

she will be blindfolded and the obstacle course rearranged. Tell him you will be his guide but will say nothing. A tap on the right or left shoulder means to go right or left. A tap on both shoulders means to go forward. A tap between the shoulders means to stop. A tap on the head means to step up. After guiding the person through, ask: *How was he able to navigate?* Conclude: *The person learned to respond to guidance.*

3. Ask: *What would have happened if we had been separated or if he had started ignoring commands?* Say: *In the same way, God guides us only when we maintain deep, abiding, current fellowship with Him.* Draw attention to the diagram on page 58 and explain the two points in "God Guides Us Only Through Maintained Fellowship with Him." Ask if anyone wants to share a testimony about the way God has guided him or her through maintained fellowship.

4. Point to the diagram on page 61. State: *The ability to have fellowship with God results from knowing His character, His purposes, and His ways.* Divide members into three groups. Ask them to use pages 62–66 to define God's character, purposes, and ways and to explain how we learn to trust God in these areas. After group work, call for reports.

5. Ask: *What changes are required to walk by faith? How does God establish a lifestyle of walking with Him by faith?* See pages 67–68.

6. Ask: *Why do people join church, then quit coming? Why do many people who attend church do so from duty or feel that* *something is missing in their lives? Part of the answer is that they don't maintain fellowship with God.* Call on the six members enlisted to present the qualities that result from consistent fellowship. Add these points:

• *God-centered vision.* Read aloud Psalm 111:10. Say: *We have correct vision when we obey Scripture; obedience creates spiritually correct understanding.*

• *Joy and gratitude.* Ask if members tried the idea in activity 20 on page 73. Thanksgiving must be personalized; we must thank God for what He has done *for us.* Ask members to give thanks to God in pairs for what He has personally done for them.

• *Responsiveness.* Summarize Paul's example. Step 1: God told Paul he would become a light to the Gentiles (see Acts 9:15). Step 2: Paul spent a year ministering in a Gentile church and became a ministry partner with Barnabas, who also had a heart for the Gentiles (see Acts 11:25-26,30). Step 3: As they were praying, the Holy Spirit sent them on a missionary journey to the Gentiles (see Acts 13:1-3).

• *Trusting God regardless of appearances.* Ask, *What would you say to help someone trust God in a difficult time?* Refer to Romans 8:28; 2 Corinthians 5:7; Hebrews 10:35-36.

• *Perseverance.* Have the group brainstorm rewards of perseverance. List responses on a dry-erase board.

7. Close by challenging members to maintain fellowship with God so that they can consistently walk by faith.

Session 4
God Requires a Faith Response to the Unveiling of His Will

Learning Goals

After the session members will be able to—
- state four foundational truths about the unveiling of God's will;
- outline a four-step process God uses to accomplish His will through believers' faith response;
- explain why remaining in the flow of a consistent walk of faith blesses others.

Before the Session

1. Read chapter 4. Complete the activities.
2. Make handouts of this true/false test.

    T F 1. God reveals His will to you, then works through you to do it.

    T F 2. Because God's will cannot be thwarted, your response does not affect whether God accomplishes His will through you.

    T F 3. Your response to the unveiling of God's will requires faith.

    T F 4. God's will is usually unveiled all at once, not one step at a time.

    T F 5. For God to unveil His will to us, we must stay in the flow of a consistent walk of faith.

3. Make a poster with the four foundational truths about the unveiling of God's will: *God first unveils His will to you. God then unveils His will through you to bless others. God unveils His will through you when you remain in the flow of a consistent walk of faith. The*

unveiling of God's will through you requires a faith response.

4. Prepare placards with the four steps God uses to accomplish His will through a faith response: *Your faith is activated by a word from God. Your faith is enacted by believing God. Your faith is visualized by watching for God. Your faith is finalized by acting on the opportunity God sets before you.*

5. Bring a lightbulb to the session.

6. Make copies of the worksheet at the top of page 154.

7. Enlist a member to present the three points in "Walking by Faith," beginning on page 99.

8. Display the poster "Stages in a Walk of Faith," used in previous sessions.

During the Session

1. Point to this week's topic on the poster "Stages in a Walk of Faith." Ask a volunteer to read the first two paragraphs of chapter 4. State: *Chapters 2–3 address God's work in us, while chapters 4–6 focus on God's work through us.*

2. Distribute true/false tests. After members complete them, show the poster with the four foundational truths about the unveiling of God's will and summarize "How God Works with Us," beginning on page 78. Refer to the diagram on page 80 to explain the third truth. Then give the answers to the test: 1. true (see Matt. 16:18); 2. false (God will accomplish His will, but He won't use you if you don't respond; see Deut. 1:35,39); 3. true (see Judg. 6:7); 4. false (recall Paul's example from ses. 3); 5. true.

The Unveiling of God's Will	Joseph's Response
1. Joseph was sold as a slave in Egypt (see Gen. 37:36).	
2. He was thrown into prison, where he interpreted the dream of the cupbearer, someone close to Pharaoh (see Gen. 39:20; 40:12-14).	
3. He interpreted Pharaoh's dream and was put him in charge of Egypt (see Gen. 41:32,40).	
4. His family came to Egypt seeking food (Gen. 42:3).	
5. He tested his brothers and discovered their remorse over selling him into slavery (Gen. 42:21-22).	

3. Point out that God accomplishes His will one step at a time as we respond in faith to each step. Explain the way God accomplished His will through the disciples as Jesus made them fishers of men (see p. 83). Call on three members to read aloud Mark 1:17-18; John 6:69; and Acts 2:41 to illustrate that process. Use Lonnie's story on pages 86–87 to illustrate what faith looks like.

4. Display placard 1: *Your faith is activated by a word from God.* Hold up the lightbulb. Ask: *When does this lightbulb come on—when it has faith that it will or when someone throws a switch?* State: *God must throw the switch to activate our faith. We do not initiate faith; we wait for Him to speak. God activates our faith by a specific word.*

5. Ask: *What does a specific word from God look like?* Have a member read Acts 16:6-10. Summarize examples from pages 84–85. Remind members that God's word often relates to people. Have a member read Acts 16:13-14. Ask: *How did Paul recognize God's leading?*

6. Point out that God's word to us may be small and subtle. Ask volunteers to share times God spoke to them subtly.

7. Display placard 2: *Your faith is enacted by believing God.* Ask a member to demonstrate his reaction if a wasp were flying around his head. State: *When we believe something, we respond. The*

154

essence of belief is acting in commitment to what we perceive to be true about God. Read aloud Luke 17:11-14 and point out that the lepers went because they believed. When God speaks, our response will reveal whether we really believe Him. Ask: *If a wasp were flying around your head, when would you respond? Likewise, the time to respond when God speaks is immediately.*

8. Display placard 3: *Your faith is visualized by watching for God.* Ask: *How do you know how to respond to God's activity?* Refer to Lonnie's story on pages 94–95. State: *We must start watching for God to put the pieces in place. Our responsibility is to look for and take appropriate action in response to God's unveiling each piece of the puzzle. Let's examine this process in Joseph's life.* Distribute copies of the worksheet you prepared. Have volunteers read the verses as the group identifies Joseph's response in each case. Make these points: *The "setbacks" positioned Joseph to visualize and receive God's will. Joseph did not know all God was doing except in retrospect, but he responded to the setbacks in faith by cheerfully serving in slavery and prison. He would have known that a correct interpretation of dreams was only from God, so he told it. He knew to save grain because God revealed it. Then he tested his brothers to learn whether they had changed their minds about him, thus making reconciliation possible. When he saw all of the pieces in place, he brought his family to Egypt.*

Encourage members to watch for God to put in place the pieces that are necessary for His will to come about and to interpret their circumstances in light of what God is doing in their lives. Call for responses to activity 18 on page 97.

9. Display placard 4: *Your faith is finalized by acting on the opportunity God sets before you.* State: *After all of the pieces were in place, Joseph was able to bring his family down to Egypt. When our faith is finalized, God completes His will through our lives.*

10. State: *To act on the opportunity God sets before you, you may have to do things you've never done before.* Call on the member enlisted to present the three points in "Walking by Faith."

11. Hold up the lightbulb and ask: *What is a lightbulb's purpose?* To provide light for people. It serves no purpose unless people are present to benefit from its light. Read aloud Genesis 12:1-3. Note that Abraham's walk of faith resulted in his being a blessing to all nations. The purposes of walking by faith are to glorify God and to bless others.

Session 5
God Matures Faith Through Waiting

Learning Goals
After the session members will be able to—
- identify purposes of waiting on God;
- state reasons waiting is the most challenging stage of faith;
- define *active seeking* and identify actions to take while waiting on God;

- name ways they will be tested while waiting;
- explain how waiting on God brings joy.

Before the Session

1. Read chapter 5. Complete the activities.
2. Bring a box wrapped in Christmas paper.
3. Prepare the following assignment slips:
   - Group 1: Genesis 6:13-14
   - Group 2: Genesis 12:2-4
   - Group 3: Genesis 37:2
   - Group 4: 1 Samuel 13:10-13
   - Group 5: 1 Samuel 16:11-12
   - Group 6: Acts 1:4-5
4. Enlist three members to summarize the actions of active seeking (pp. 113–15).
5. Make copies of the worksheet at the bottom of this page.
6. Display the poster "Stages in a Walk of Faith," used in previous sessions.

During the Session

1. Hold up the Christmas box and point out that when we were growing up, we had to wait for Christmas to open our presents. A walk of faith also requires waiting. Point to this session's topic on the poster "Stages in a Walk of Faith."

2. Divide members into six groups and give each group an assignment slip. Ask the groups to read the Scripture and to identify the biblical characters, the word from God, and the length of their wait. Allow time for work; then call for reports. Answers are at the top of page 157. Point out that after God gives us a specific word, we may experience a period of waiting until He fulfills it.

3. Ask the group why God might require us to wait. Record ideas on a dry-erase board. Then point out the four purposes of waiting on page 103. Ask members to identify the purposes of waiting for the biblical characters they examined. Summarize: *God is not on a speed timetable but a character timetable.*

4. State: *Waiting on God is the most challenging part of walking by faith.* Ask for responses to activity 3 on page 105. Ask: *Why is waiting so hard for us?*

5. State: *To wait on God, we must reject the tendency to walk by sight.* Ask a member to read aloud 2 Corinthians 5:7. Ask: *Why do we find it easier to walk by sight?* Present the four ideas on pages 108–9 and ask members which influences make it hard for them to walk by faith.

Actions of Active Seeking	An Example from Your Life
1. Ask until you have clarity.	
2. Seek specifically and expectantly.	
3. As you knock, keep doing what God has called you to do.	

Biblical Character	Word from God	Length of Wait
1. Noah	Build an ark	Perhaps 120 years
2. Abraham	Make him a great nation, beginning with a son	25 years until a son came
3. Joseph	Rule over family	22 years
4. Saul	Sacrifice before battle	Seven days
5. David	Become king	More than 20 years
6. 11 disciples	Receive the Holy Spirit	10 or 11 days

6. Ask: *What do you think Paul had to do to reject walking by sight?* Explain: *We must learn to live with an unmet need or desire.* Ask members to name examples of living with unmet needs. Instruct them to write down their most challenging unmet need. Ask: *Are you willing to live with it for as long as it takes for God to fulfill His purposes in you and in others?* Point out the lessons Lonnie learned from a period of waiting (pp. 111–12).

7. Ask: *What are we supposed to do while waiting on God?* After responses, write the term *active seeking* on a dry-erase board. Ask: *How does active seeking differ from waiting, for example, at the doctor's office?* State: *Waiting on God is an active process requiring action.*

8. Call on the three members enlisted to summarize the actions of active seeking. Then use the examples at the top of page 158 to illustrate the three actions.

9. Distribute copies of the worksheet and ask members to complete them.

10. Assign members to read aloud the following verses: Deuteronomy 8:2; Judges 2:22; 1 Chronicles 29:17; 2 Chronicles 32:31; Psalm 11:4; Jeremiah 17:10; John 6:6. Point out that after receiving a word from God, we are often tested.

11. Divide members into five groups. Assign each group one of the tests on pages 117–22. Ask them to review the assigned section, be prepared to report on it, and identify ways to remain faithful when tested this way. Allow time for groups to work; then call for reports.

12. Read aloud James 1:2-3. Point out that these verses connect joy to waiting. State: *We can have joy during waiting because we can anticipate with confidence that God will develop Christlikeness in us and will bring about what He has promised.*

Actions of Active Seeking	Paul's Example	Lonnie's Example
1. Ask until you have clarity.	General word: plant Gentile churches. Specific word: "Don't preach in Asia. Don't preach in Bythinia. Preach in Macedonia" (see Acts 16:6-10).	Prayed for housing. Initially asked for 12-room house, later for $85,000 for hospital.
2. Seek specifically and expectantly.	Go to place of prayer. Witness to Lydia. Still watched to see what God would do (see Acts 16:13-15).	Committed to buy hospital. Starting looking for God to provide resources.
3. As you knock, keep doing what God has called you to do.	Cast out demon (see Acts 16:18). Thrown in prison (see v. 23). Still testified (see v. 25). Jailer converted (see vv. 31-34). Church results (see Letter to the Philippians).	Ministered while staying in empty basements, apartments, and houses for two years.

Chapter 6
God Rewards Completed Faith

Learning Goals

After the session members will be able to—
- give biblical evidence that God rewards completed faith;
- state four conditions of God's rewards;
- identify rewards of completed faith in the kingdom and in their lives;
- name rewards of incomplete faith;
- affirm that completed faith leads to opportunities for greater service.

Before the Session

1. Read chapter 6. Complete the activities.
2. Prepare a minilecture on the four conditions of God's rewards on pages 126–32. Make placards with the four rewards.

3. Bring a medal or trophy to the session.
4. Have paper and pencils or pens.
5. Display the poster "Stages in a Walk of Faith," used in previous sessions.

During the Session

1. Ask: *Who would like to get rich?* State that you know how members can gain riches that will never be at risk. Call on members to read aloud Matthew 6:1,4,6,18,20. Point out that four times Jesus spoke of getting a reward and even commanded us in verse 20 to collect treasures. God wants to reward us, and the rewards will be eternal.
2. Show the medal or trophy and state: *Winning a reward requires competing by the rules. God's rewards also have conditions. Each reward in Matthew 6*

comes with a condition. Display the four placards you made as you present a minilecture on the four conditions of God's rewards on pages 126–32.

3. Ask: *When a player competes and wins, what does he expect his team to receive? What kind of reward do you expect to get when you walk by faith?* Say: *God gives three kingdom rewards.* Ask three members to read aloud Matthew 5:16; Acts 9:31; Acts 2:41. After each verse is read, write on a dry-erase board: *God is glorified. The church is edified. Humanity is redeemed.* Explain: *These kingdom rewards, in large measure, will compose your spiritual obituary when you die. Angels and believers will celebrate how God glorified Himself, strengthened the church, and/or redeemed others through you. Mature faith perceives the greatest reward as being a servant through whom others are influenced.*

4. Ask: *When Joseph served Potiphar and the prison keeper, whom did it benefit—them or Joseph?* Both. God uses your faith to bless you and others simultaneously. Divide members into four groups and assign each group one of the rewards on pages 138–43. Ask the groups to review the assigned topic and to summarize the reward for the large group, including a biblical example. After the groups report, ask volunteers to share ways they have already experienced these rewards of completed faith.

5. Ask: *If we quit before the game is over, what is the reward of our practice and hard work?* Ask a member to read aloud Hebrews 10:32-38. State: *If we start*

well but don't finish, we don't receive the reward. Ask: *What are the rewards of incomplete faith?* List responses on a dry-erase board. Review pages 143–45.

6. Read aloud Romans 1:17 and point out the relational nature of faith. God moves us from faith to faith as we respond to His activity in our lives. Ask: *How would you chart the progression of God's work in David's life?* Draw a timeline on a dry-erase board and label it as volunteers respond. Then follow the same process with Paul. Possible answers are provided in the final paragraph on page 145. State: *David and Paul's obedience in faith opened the door to greater opportunities of service and blessing.*

7. Distribute paper and pencils or pens. Instruct members to chart the progression of God's work in their lives as they have responded in faith.

8. Challenge members to allow God to use them to make an impact on their world as they walk by faith in Him.

1. Michelangelo, "Confidence," *Wisdom for the Soul* [online] 2004 [cited 13 July 2006]. Available from the Internet: *www.geocities.com/wisdomforthesoul/categories/confidence.html.*

2. Unsolicited letter received by John Franklin.

3. Archie Bunker, "Faith" [online; cited 11 July 2006]. Available from the Internet: *www.nowscape.com/mormon/faith_def.htm.*

4. Mary Baker Eddy, *Science and Health with Key to the Scriptures* (Boston, 1934), 497:5.

5. Charles Capps, in Gary Gilley, "The Word-Faith Movement" [online; cited 11 July 2006]. Available from the Internet: *www.rapidnet.com/~jbeard/bdm/Psychology/char/more/w-f.htm.*

6. George Bernard Shaw, in Jone Johnson Lewis, "Wisdom Quotes: Quotations to Inspire and Challenge" [online], 1995–2006 [cited 11 July 2006]. Available from the Internet: *www.wisdomquotes.com/cat_faith.html.*

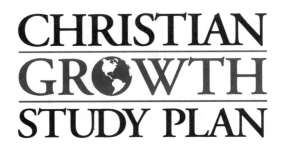

CHRISTIAN GROWTH STUDY PLAN

In the Christian Growth Study Plan *By Faith: Living in the Certainty of God's Reality* is a resource for course credit in the subject area Bible Studies in the Christian Growth category of diploma plans. To receive credit, read the book; complete the learning activities; attend group sessions; show your work to your pastor, a staff member, or a church leader; then complete the form. This page may be duplicated. Send the completed form to:

Christian Growth Study Plan
One LifeWay Plaza; Nashville, TN 37234-0117
Fax (615) 251-5067; e-mail *cgspnet@lifeway.com*
For information about the Christian Growth Study Plan, refer to the current *Christian Growth Study Plan Catalog*, located online at *www.lifeway.com/cgsp*. If you do not have access to the Internet, contact the Christian Growth Study Plan office, (800) 968-5519, for the specific plan you need.

BY FAITH
COURSE NUMBER: CG-1193

PARTICIPANT INFORMATION

Social Security Number (USA ONLY-optional)	Personal CGSP Number*	Date of Birth (MONTH, DAY, YEAR)
– –	– –	– –

Name (First, Middle, Last)		Home Phone
		– –

Address (Street, Route, or P.O. Box)	City, State, or Province	Zip/Postal Code

Email Address for CGSP use

Please check appropriate box: ❑ Resource purchased by church ❑ Resource purchased by self ❑ Other

CHURCH INFORMATION

Church Name

Address (Street, Route, or P.O. Box)	City, State, or Province	Zip/Postal Code

CHANGE REQUEST ONLY

☐ Former Name

☐ Former Address	City, State, or Province	Zip/Postal Code

☐ Former Church	City, State, or Province	Zip/Postal Code

Signature of Pastor, Conference Leader, or Other Church Leader	Date

*New participants are requested but not required to give SS# and date of birth. Existing participants, please give CGSP# when using SS# for the first time. Thereafter, only one ID# is required. **Mail to:** Christian Growth Study Plan, One LifeWay Plaza, Nashville, TN 37234-0117. Fax: (615)251-5067.

Revised 4-05